A VIEW FROM THE
EYE OF THE STORM

A VIEW FROM THE EYE OF THE STORM

TERROR AND REASON IN THE MIDDLE EAST

HAIM HARARI

10 ReganBooks
Celebrating Ten Bestselling Years
An Imprint of HarperCollins*Publishers*

A hardcover edition of this book was published in 2005 by ReganBooks, an imprint of HarperCollins Publishers.

HarperCollins books may be purchased for educational, business, or sales promotional use. For information please write: Special Markets Department, HarperCollins Publishers Inc., 10 East 53rd Street, New York, NY 10022.

First paperback edition published 2005.

Designer: Publications Development Company

Library of Congress Cataloging-in-Publication Data for the hardcover edition has been applied for.

ISBN 0-06-083912-0 (pbk.)

05 06 07 08 09 PDC/RRD 10 9 8 7 6 5 4 3 2 1

To Elfi, who gallantly walked into the storm
and weathered it.

CONTENTS

Apologies   ix

Foreword: The Scientist and the Taxi Driver   xi

— PART I —
The Raging Storm

1	From Abraham Lincoln to the Internet	3
2	Where Is the Storm?	11
3	MTA: Master's in Terror Administration	17
4	The Virgins Are Ready	23
5	A Ticking Bomb	29
6	Rewriting International Law	33
7	The Referee Is Biased	39

— PART II —
The Hesitant World

8	Trouble in Globania	47
9	Intellectual Property and Intellectual Poverty	53
10	There Goes the Neighborhood	57
11	The Non-Arab Crescent	65
12	Freedom Fries	71
13	Does the Sun Rise in the East	79
14	Right Is Wrong	87
15	Left Behind	91
16	Ignorance and Apathy	97

— PART III —
The Persistent Lies

17 The Superficial Village   105
18 Words Kill   113
19 Pictures Lie   121
20 The Truth, but Not the Whole Truth   129
21 Some Refugees Are More Equal than Others   137
22 Rewriting History   143
23 Life Near the End Zone   151
24 Fooling Most of the People, Most of the Time   159

— Intermezzo: "They" —   165

— PART IV —
The Uncertain Future

25 They Mean What They Say   169
26 Why Don't You Choose Someone Else?   175
27 Milli-Globania in the Eye of the Storm   181
28 Collective Suicide   185
29 Everybody Knows the Solution   191
30 The Nuclear Stone Age   195
31 A Correct Diagnosis Is Half a Cure   201
32 The World According to My Grandmother   207
Acknowledgments   213
Index   215

APOLOGIES

I apologize to the victims of terror for occasionally using humor in this book. The subject is not funny at all, but part of what has kept the Jews alive for centuries is the ability to laugh and smile in difficult times. I see no reason to allow the terrorists to spoil this tradition.

I apologize to all scholars in fields such as history, politics, Middle Eastern affairs, international relations, journalism, and international law, as well as to the practitioners of many other professions—including all proverbial taxi drivers—for invading their territory in such an amateurish manner. I certainly would not like them to write books about my own field, theoretical physics. My only defense is that they have not been forced to live through, and think about, theoretical physics every single day since they were born.

I apologize for not including in this book elaborate footnotes and many pages of references to official documents and academic papers. This is not a scholarly book. It is an attempt to present the common sense view of one citizen who cares.

I apologize for any errors in presenting facts. I did my best to check and double check, but I may have slipped somewhere. I guarantee that my record in this matter is far above the average for writers on the subject, who interchange fact and fiction so often. But this is not good enough. I hope I have done much better. But only the Pope is infallible, and even he cannot order the storm to stop.

I apologize for the short quotations at the beginning of every chapter. I could not resist them. Please blame me for all of them, unless you discover that someone else said the same thing, many years ago. If so, I was not aware of it, but I here and now abandon any pride of authorship.

I apologize if I have been insensitive in describing an issue or in referring to any group of people. I have done my best to avoid this, but the subject was so full of emotion that it would be a miracle if I had succeeded. Terrorists, and all those who help them, knowingly or otherwise, are exempted from this apology.

Finally, I apologize to any critics, who may wish to review this book, for invading their territory as well, by offering them in these apologies enough material for a passable book review.

FOREWORD: THE SCIENTIST AND THE TAXI DRIVER

It was a cold winter evening in Vienna in the late 1990s. I got into a taxi and gave the address to the driver. All I spoke were two words: a street name and one digit. I thought I pronounced them properly. The driver turned to me and said, "*Beseder*," meaning "all is in order."

"How did you know that I speak Hebrew?" I asked.

"One word was enough for me. I recognized your accent," he said in Hebrew, with a strong Arabic accent. He was a Palestinian from Hebron, he told me; after the 1967 Six-Day War he had worked for years in Jerusalem, becoming a very close friend of his Jewish employer and his family. Twenty years later, while still working for the same employer, he decided to start a new life and moved to Vienna to drive a taxi. It took him all of three minutes to start giving me his "view from the eye of the storm."

"It is all the fault of the fanatics and the crazies on both sides," he said. "We, the simple people, love one another and do not want any violence. I liked my Jewish employer, and he liked me. Our families were close. We wanted peace and quiet. We should treat everybody in a nice way, on both sides."

I relaxed in the back seat of the taxi. "A real peace-loving Palestinian," I thought. For a few minutes we were in "love thy neighbor, and be nice to everybody" territory. And then he announced: "I will tell you how to solve the problem. Line up all the fanatics and the crazies from both sides, facing a wall. Take a submachine gun, and shoot them all dead."

Not possessing a clear logical or legal definition of "fanatics" and "crazies," I remained silent until we reached our destination. I tipped him generously, he said shalom, and we gave each other a friendly smile.

The proverbial taxi driver is a well-known mythological figure. But real live taxi drivers also exist. There are also real live scientists and proverbial ones. If you had to invent a theatrical encounter between a real Israeli scientist and a proverbial Palestinian taxi driver, you could not have selected a better scene. Reality is often more creative than any playwright.

The proverbial scientist has a sky-high IQ. He is often lost in his scientific thoughts and forgets where he is. He makes great discoveries while shaving. He often uses terminology that almost no one understands. He cares more about DNA than about the NBA and thinks that the Beatles are insects. He knows that everything is complicated. His logic is impeccable, but his common sense is not.

Most real scientists are not at all proverbial.

The proverbial taxi driver always knows where he is. He understands people from all walks of life and has opinions about everything. He may think that a microchip is a small fried potato and that the big bang is the car accident he witnessed yesterday. He has no need to be politically correct, and he never hesitates to express views on topics that are none of his business. His common sense is impeccable, but his logic is not.

Most real taxi drivers are not at all proverbial.

I am a real scientist, not at all proverbial. I know that applying pure logic to real-life situations is sometimes useful but often dangerous. I am definitely not a real taxi driver, although at age five I dreamed of becoming the driver of a double-decker bus. But I have always tried to apply the commonsense, tell-it-like-it-is attitude of the proverbial taxi driver to most problems of everyday life, issues requiring vision, and attempts at predicting the future.

I believe that, when a real scientist wishes to express his views on topics that are none of his professional business, he should try to do so as if he were a proverbial taxi driver. This book is a modest attempt to do just that.

PART I

THE RAGING STORM

─1─

FROM ABRAHAM LINCOLN
TO THE INTERNET

The first Internet line outside the United States linked the United States to Italy and Israel. Had it happened 130 years earlier, my great-grandmother could have sent e-mails from Jerusalem to Lincoln and Garibaldi.

My grandmother Sarah (same name as the biblical wife of Abraham) was born in Jerusalem in 1872, when Queen Victoria, Emperor Franz Josef, and Otto von Bismarck were in the news. My great-grandmother Yocheved (same name as the biblical mother of Moses) was also born in Jerusalem. She was eight years old when Abraham Lincoln became president. Her own mother was also born in Jerusalem at a time when California still belonged to Mexico and Garibaldi had not yet liberated Italy.

My four grandchildren, all of whom were born in Israel and live there today, are seventh-generation Israeli born. For seven generations we have lived here, in the eye of the storm. We have survived more wars and terror attacks than any other nation. But now we are informed by the former French ambassador to London that we are "a shitty little country" endangering the world; at the same time, we learn that the rulers of Iran want to replace our "shitty little country" with yet another Shiite country.

My mother, Dina (same name as the biblical daughter of Jacob), was eighty-two years old when Saddam Hussein sent his Scud missiles into the center of Tel Aviv in 1991. She lived in a fourth-floor apartment there, but did not go to a shelter and refused to put on her gas mask. "I survived World War I, the deportation of the Jews of Tel Aviv to Damascus, the first wave of Arab terror [or intifada] in 1921, the second one in 1929, the third in 1936 to 1939, World War II, the War of Independence and the Egyptian bombing of Tel Aviv in 1948, the 1956 Sinai War, the 1967 Six-Day War, the 1973 Yom Kippur War, and all the terror attacks in between," she said. "I am not going to get excited about Saddam."

As a scientist and educator, I travel frequently around the world, lecturing on topics of science, technology, and education, almost always avoiding discussions about the Middle East and the world around us. Why should I concentrate on painful issues when science is so exciting and education so rewarding? If you live in a constantly stormy area and you visit a calm resort, would you want to discuss the weather?

But in my travels I could not avoid detecting an incredible amount of ignorance regarding all matters related to our region of the world. I can understand disputes about opinions and views when the facts are known. I can even accept minor twists in describing facts; history is not an exact science. We also know about Rashomon: Different witnesses to the same event may tell different stories. But I cannot think of any other topic about which so much disinformation has been spread for so many years, by so many people, in so many places. An amazing number of educated and intelligent people have fallen victim to distortions, misconceptions, and pure unadulterated lies. And when you point out some simple undisputed facts, the response is always the same: "How come nobody told me?"

As long as the Cold War was dominating international politics, our own little corner of the world may have been a perennial trouble spot, but no one would even dream of blaming it for every evil under the sun. With the collapse of one superpower and the emerging threat of global terror, the large region from Morocco to Indonesia, or at least from Algeria to Pakistan, has become the principal theater in a very ugly drama. The Israeli-Arab conflict, while continuing to simmer and sometimes boil, is only a minor part of the scene, but that does not prevent many from blaming every piece of bad news, as usual, on Israel and the Jews.

Some people make such claims as a result of old-fashioned or newly crafted anti-Semitic attitudes. But most are the victims of a massive disinformation campaign. In addition to being fed a rich diet of lies, these people observe each new outrageous act of terror from a rather naive, sterile, and civilized point of view. It is noble to turn the other cheek, but not when you are facing someone who wants to kidnap you and cut off your head. To use civilized standards based on legal arguments when judging suicide murders or the use of children as human shields is an equally big mistake. It has been pointed out long ago that idealism increases in direct proportion to the distance from the danger, but the danger is now everywhere.

I have spent many years performing scientific research in the United States and quite a number of years in Europe. My wife is European and my non-Israeli friends are equally divided between Europe and the United States. I have my own list of what I like and dislike about the two sides of the Atlantic. Israel itself has many Middle Eastern features, but it also has strong influences from both Europe and America. In addition to loving my own country, I do love America and I do love Europe. If there were such a thing as a global passport, I would be proud to hold one in addition to my Israeli passport. All of these feelings color my view from the eye of the storm.

There is no reason that you should care about my political views. This book is not at all about them. But I want to live, and I want my children and grandchildren to live. I also want Israel to live, and I want everybody else in the Middle East to live in dignity—unless they deliberately want to murder me. These wishes do not make me a fanatic, right-wing zealot. Actually, anyone who knows me would place me somewhere a few centimeters left of center, on any reasonable scale. I am in favor of compromises, I am against any nation dominating another, and I simply cannot wait for the day when peace will come to the Middle East. But, unlike certain other people in the greater Middle East, I am not suicidal.

I believe that the number one priority of the human race is to educate and advance the billions who are uneducated, poor, hungry, and sick. But this does not mean being soft on hostage takers, suicide murderers, throat cutters, inciting pathological liars, and those who finance them, train them, and lead them. In fact, as long as these characters are around, the uneducated poor masses will never move forward.

When I meet new people outside of Israel, they often ask me: "Where are you from?" I answer that I am an Israeli. "Yes, but where did you originally come from?" I say: "I was born in Jerusalem in 1940." "Yes, but where did your parents come from?" Well, both were born in Jaffa in 1908, and both moved into Tel Aviv one year later, when their two families were among the sixty founding families of the new city in the sands. The interrogation usually continues until we reach my great-great-grandmother, who was also born in Jerusalem, and then I hear: "Your family must have been one of the few Jewish families in Arab Palestine."

I'm then obliged to spoil the fun by pointing out that in 1844, my great-great-grandmother was one of the 16,270 inhabitants of Jerusalem counted by the Ottoman Empire when it performed its first census. The Ottomans found in Jerusalem 7,120 Jews, 5,760 Muslims, and 3,390 Christians. To be sure, my great-great-grandmother was one of few Jews in Jerusalem, but there were even fewer Muslims. "Jerusalem was not then the capital city of anything, but it was one of several main little towns in the Syrian province of the Ottoman Empire," I add. In fact, in the past three thousand years, Jerusalem has never been the capital city to anyone except the ancient Jews and the modern Jews. In hundreds of years of Muslim control of Jerusalem, it was never the capital.

"I thought that Jerusalem was in Palestine, not in Syria," is the next remark I usually hear from the well-meaning, educated European or American, forcing me to explain that, in fact, "Palestine" as a unified separate political entity, independent or otherwise, sovereign or otherwise, did not exist in the last two thousand years, until the British conquest at the end of World War I. Until then the area was part of the Syrian province of the Ottoman Empire, covering the entire area between Turkey and Egypt. For centuries, different rulers governed it, creating a variety of provinces, boundaries, and subdivisions. Modern Syria, Lebanon, Jordan, and Israel are all new subdivisions introduced by the colonial British and French after World War I.

At this point, I begin to detect disbelief. "You mean to say that the Palestinians did not own and run this flourishing country for centuries?" They certainly did not. It was always owned and ruled by those who conquered it from the outside. The last sovereign state here, before the State of Israel, was the ancient Jewish state, two thousand years ago. And if, in 1844, one of the main "cities" had a population of 16,000 or so, it is pretty clear that the country was almost empty, by any European standard. It was not empty by the standards of the nineteenth-century Middle East. There was a village here and there, minimal agriculture, lots of swamps in the low areas, bare mountains, olive trees, desert, and "cities" of 20,000 people or so. This was, presumably, very much like the rest of Syria, Lebanon, Jordan, Iraq, and everywhere else in that part of the world.

To say that nearly forty years of conversations like these disturbed me is an understatement. I was often upset, and sometimes amazed, by the successful penetration of so much fiction into the facts of the Middle East. Scientists aren't normally forced to deal with such matters. We are trained to deal with facts, not with fiction. We also know that if someone in the world of science is caught even once in a deliberate lie, he or she is entirely excluded, forever, from the scientific community; no scientist would ever listen to or employ him or her again.

There were also claims and arguments that I heard from my own countrymen that annoyed me. "There is no such thing as a Palestinian people," some said, including the late Golda Meir. Of course there is. A clear Palestinian Arab identity has been created during the past one hundred years, mainly due to the conflict with the Jews. The Palestinians today are clearly a well-defined national group, even if they were not so a century ago. Another claim is that "Israel is entitled to build villages and towns, wherever it wishes, among the Palestinian towns." Of course this should not be done, especially if the main purpose is to annoy the local population, humiliate it, and deny it its own development.

As a scientist, I am a member of several international bodies, committees, and advisory boards. In some of them, I am the only scientist. In others, I am the only Israeli. It was almost accidental that I was asked, as the only Middle Eastern member of one such board, to present my own personal view from the eye of the storm.

I chose to discuss the problem of terrorism and the crisis in the Muslim world, not concentrating on the Israeli-Palestinian conflict. My remarks were not to have been published; I gave the report in a closed meeting, and only the participants themselves received it in written form. I did not even dream of circulating the text of my lecture. How it happened and why, I do not know, but someone obviously leaked the piece. Within a couple of months it had found its way, under various unauthorized titles, into more than a thousand websites around the world. I have received reactions from all directions. It was printed without permission in an obscure local newspaper in the United States and quoted by prominent international columnists. I received messages from places like Australia, Sweden, and El Salvador. A Portuguese translation arrived from Rio de Janeiro, along with unauthorized translations into Dutch, French, German, Italian, Hebrew, and Spanish. In hundreds of e-mails from strangers, I received endless requests to permit further dissemination, in one form or another, all of which I turned down.

My speech did not include any new data or privileged information. I simply told it like it was, evaluating the situation as well as I could, from my own personal point of view—as a "proverbial taxi driver," not as a scientist. Scientists, after all, are no better qualified than taxi drivers to express views on such matters. I am not a historian, a professional expert on Middle East affairs, or a politician; I am not even a journalist. I will never be any of the above.

Nevertheless, some of the websites devoted serious discussion to various aspects of my article. Several patterns amazed me. There was relatively little criticism, even though it dealt with such a controversial and emotional topic. One of the first rebuttals I found was a one-liner; it reminded me of the old saying, "Profanity is a compromise between fighting it out and running away."

It seemed that most of the readers were already "believers" in much of what I said and that the wealth of good and bad stuff on the Internet led people to read mostly what "their kind of people" wrote. This was disappointing. I certainly hope that the present book will be read by skeptics, and not just by those who identify with my views.

Another bizarre pattern emerged in quite a few websites. People wrote: "I wonder if this is not a hoax written by someone else. If it is really written by Haim Harari, it is extremely interesting and eye-opening." Clearly none of these people knew who Haim Harari was. Why would it matter who wrote it? Others wrote things like, "I wonder if this guy is a Rightist. If so, the article is one-sided. But if he is not, it is a stunning and illuminating analysis of the situation." The possibility that someone might write such an article and claim to be me is absurd. The idea that you are suspected of being a Rightist because you oppose terror, or that you have to be a non-Rightist for your words to count, is perhaps an indicator of the intellectual integrity of many who read (and write) about the subject.

The one lesson I took away from this Internet experience is this: If you have something to say in public, make sure you control where, how, and why it is published. If you don't have anything to say, the least you can do is shut up.

Having encountered lies and disinformation throughout the forty years I've spent traveling around the world, I've been convinced by my family history and life experience that I have something to say. My long career of presenting science to the general public tells me that you should always explain your views in simple terms, using familiar everyday analogies, without trying to impress anyone with your deep professional expertise, even if you have it. Hence, "a view from the eye of the storm," offered by an Israeli scientist, is from the viewpoint of a proverbial taxi driver.

— 2 —

WHERE IS THE STORM?

If you draw a map of all the Arab states, covering the entire front page of the New York Times, *Israel would cover less that the single letter "N" in the name of the newspaper.*

There are twenty-two Arab countries in the world. The total land area they cover is more than 5 million square miles or 13 million square kilometers—much larger than all of Europe, from the Ural to the Atlantic. The area covered by Israel is about half of that of Slovakia. The Arab lands are much larger than the entire territory of the United States, including Alaska. Israel is a little larger than Hawaii. The twenty-two Arab states have a population of more than three hundred million people, with almost no Jews left. Israel has six million, of which more than one million are Arabs.

The world seems to be obsessed with Israel. Many Europeans support the Arabs because they are "the underdog." Did I hear that right? The underdog? How can 6 million people endanger 300 million? Could Slovakia trouble Russia, Germany, France, Britain, Italy, and all the rest of Europe combined? Could Hawaii threaten the entire United States? Excuse the expression, but this is total nonsense.

I could have begun by sharing with you some fascinating facts and personal thoughts about the Israeli-Arab conflict. However, I prefer to devote my first remarks to the broader picture of the Arab world and its contiguous Muslim countries. I refer to the entire area between Pakistan and Morocco, which is predominantly Arab and Muslim, but includes many non-Arab and also significant non-Muslim minorities. This is where the storm is, even if Israel is in its eye.

Why put aside Israel and its own immediate neighborhood, even temporarily? Because Israel and its problems, in spite of what you might read or hear in the world media, are not the central issue, and never have been, in the upheaval in the region. Yes, there is a hundred-year-old Israeli-Arab conflict, but that's not where the main show is.

The millions who died in the Iran-Iraq War had nothing to do with Israel. The mass murder happening right now in Sudan, where the Arab Muslim regime is massacring its black Christian citizens in the south and its Muslim citizens in the west, has nothing to do with Israel. The frequent reports from Algeria about the murders of hundreds of civilians in one village or another by other Algerians have nothing to do with Israel. The hundreds of insurgents killed recently in Yemen, the Saudis killed by al Qaida and the Muslim-Christian civil war in Lebanon, were not triggered by Israel. Saddam Hussein did not invade Kuwait, endanger Saudi Arabia, and butcher his own people because of Israel. He alone killed many more Iraqis than the total number of casualties of all the Israeli-Arab clashes over one hundred years, on both sides. Are these lives less important? Egypt did not use poison gas against Yemen in the 1960s because of Israel. Assad the father did not kill tens of thousands of his own citizens in one week in El Hamma in Syria because of Israel. The Taliban control of Afghanistan and the civil war there had nothing to do with Israel. Libya's bombing of Pan Am 103 had nothing to do with Israel. I could go on and on.

The root of the trouble is that the entire Muslim region itself is dysfunctional, by any standard of the word, and would have been so even if Israel would have joined the Arab league and an independent Palestine had existed for one hundred years. The twenty-two Arab countries, from Mauritania to the Gulf States, have a population larger than that of the United States and almost as large as the European Union before its recent expansion. These countries, with all their oil and natural resources, have a combined Gross Domestic Product (GDP) smaller than that of the Netherlands plus Belgium and equal to half of the GDP of California alone. Within this meager GDP, the gaps between rich and poor are beyond belief, and too many of the rich have made their money not by succeeding in business, but by being corrupt rulers or by depositing the oil money in very few pockets. The social status of women is far below what it was in the Western world one hundred and fifty years ago. Women are not allowed to drive a car in Saudi Arabia. Women who are raped usually find themselves accused of damaging the honor of their families, an act punishable by death for the woman, not her rapist. Human rights are below any reasonable standard, in spite of the grotesque fact that Libya was elected to chair the United Nations Human Rights Commission.

According to a report prepared by a committee of Arab intellectuals and published under the auspices of the UN, the number of books translated by the entire Arab world is much smaller than what little Greece alone translates. The total number of scientific publications of 300 million Arabs is less than that of 6 million Israelis. Birth rates in the region are very high, increasing the region's poverty, social inequality, and cultural decline. And all of this is happening in a region that was being touted only thirty years ago as the next wealthy part of the world, one that has historically been one of the most advanced cultures in the world.

It is fair to say that these factors have conspired to create an unprecedented breeding ground for cruel dictators, terror networks, fanaticism, incitement, abductions and beheading, suicide murders, and general decline. It is also a fact that almost everybody in the region blames this situation on the United States, on Israel, on Western civilization, on Judaism and Christianity, or on anyone and anything except themselves.

Do I say all of this with the satisfaction of someone discussing the failings of his enemies? On the contrary: I firmly believe that the world would be a much better place if things were different. I believe that the Western world must do everything possible to help educate the Arab masses, gain rights for Muslim women, and help create a decent Arab judicial system. This may sound paternalistic, and some Arab leaders would claim that it would represent a colonialist invasion of values. But the alternatives are either a gradual move toward a World War III, eventually leading to a Muslim defeat, or a Muslim Europe, pushing the region back in time to earlier centuries.

There are many millions of decent, honest, good people who are either devout Muslims or secular citizens raised in Muslim families. They are double victims—of an outside world that is now developing "Islamophobia," and of their own environment, which breaks their hearts with its cruel dysfunction. The vast silent majority of these Muslims are not part of the terror and incitement, but the problem is that they do not stand up against it. In maintaining their silence, they become accomplices by omission. This applies equally to political leaders, intellectuals, businesspeople, and others throughout the Muslim world. Many of them certainly know right from wrong but are afraid to express their views.

History is full of examples of evil leaders who destroyed entire nations, mostly their own, because the silent majority of decent and fair-minded people were numb, fearful, and coerced into collaborating. It is not easy for such people to stand up against terror and incitement, especially when they are continuously brainwashed by lies and fabrications. But the fate of hundreds of millions of Muslims depends first and foremost on the liberation of this silent majority from its chains of submission.

The persistent ugly storm engulfing the Arab world is at the root of the current world conflict—the conflict we might already think of as an undeclared World War III. A few more years may pass before everybody acknowledges that this is a world war, but we are already well into it. It rages from Bali to Madrid, from Nairobi to New York, from Buenos Aires to Istanbul, and from Tunis to Moscow. Iraq, the Palestinian area, Saudi Arabia, and Afghanistan are just some of the favorite spots of the dysfunctional players, but they are definitely not the full story.

— 3 —

MTA: MASTER'S IN TERROR ADMINISTRATION

When al Qaida, Hamas, Islamic Jihad, and Hizbullah go public on NASDAQ, we will know more about their operations. For now, they are listed only in the Teheran and Damascus emerging markets.

Western democracy is considered the least bad of modern political systems. It is not only a form of government, but also a way of life. When you grow up in such a democratic society, even if you are a complete atheist, you take for granted religious freedom, sanctity of places of worship, and respect for religious leaders. You grow up in a world blessed by free speech, free international travel, and voluntary organizations dedicated to social welfare and education. You know that everyone is innocent until proven guilty, and you believe in human rights, not only of your dear friends, but also of suspected murderers, drug dealers, and leaders of organized crime. A necessary component of democracy is a free press — including the electronic media, which tell any story with pictures, known to be more effective than a thousand words, and cover complicated issues with short sound bites. There is much to improve in our political system, but it is the best we have, so far.

Yet such systems have their limitations. Every student of political science debates how an antidemocratic force can be prevented from winning a democratic election and abolishing democracy. Other aspects of civilized society are open to question: Can a policeman open fire on an armed robber who might otherwise kill him? Should a government have the right to listen to the phone conversations of drug dealers? Does free speech protect your right to shout "fire" in a crowded theater? Should openly racist political parties be outlawed? Should incitement to murder a democratically elected political leader be protected by free speech? These are old-fashioned dilemmas. Countless articles and books have been devoted to each of them.

But now there is another virtual book being outlined, chapter by chapter, step by step, by many people around the world. It might be called *How to Use the Tools of Democracy Against It Most Effectively.* This is the mandatory text for anyone working toward a master's in terror administration, the MTA degree offered by the university of real life. Certain chapters of this collective effort have actually been published in various websites related to al Qaida and Hizbullah.

As in any other business organization, everything in this effort is propelled by money. There are three concentric spheres supporting death and murder. In the inner circle are the terrorists themselves—the ones who kill, kidnap, hijack, behead victims, slash throats, and blow themselves up. The money funds their travel, explosives, hideouts, and permanent search for soft, vulnerable targets.

These are surrounded by a second, wider circle of direct supporters, planners, commanders, and preachers, all of whom make a living—usually a very comfortable one—by serving as terror infrastructure. Finally, a third circle of so-called religious, educational, and welfare organizations, which actually do some good by feeding the hungry and educating the young, but that nevertheless help to brainwash a new generation with hatred, lies, and ignorance.

The third circle operates mostly through mosques, madrassas, and other religious establishments, but also through the electronic and printed media. It is this circle that ensures that women will continue to be treated as inferior and that the children of the next generation will also be raised on hatred. It also enforces the idea that democracy is unthinkable and that exposure to the outside world is forbidden. Finally, this outer circle leads the way in blaming everybody outside the Muslim world for the miseries of its people.

This business plan is ingenious. If such incitement were propagated through any vehicle, other than religious institutions and the media, it would be easy to stop it. But no Western democracy would dare to censor the words of a Friday preacher in a mosque, curtail the freedom of the press to incite listeners, or block satellite TV broadcasts. Even less democratic countries would think twice before they would outlaw certain "religious services." The religious preachers themselves can always claim the right to free speech, and other than spreading hatred, they are generally careful not to violate any laws.

Lax immigration laws, based on decency and fairness to asylum seekers, are exploited shamelessly by those who would spread terror. Hospitality to foreign students and free international travel provide additional tools. Fund-raising for educational and social goals for the poor masses of the Islamic world is definitely a noble task. Controlling how such money is spent, of course, is another matter. If you contribute to the cause of educating Arab children and the money ends up funding a summer terror camp for ten-year-old potential suicide bombers, too bad. If you contribute to the welfare of low-income people and the money flows to the families of murderers, you are inadvertently supporting mass murder. In all cases, your contributions are tax deductible—meaning that Uncle Sam, too, may be unknowingly paying for the terror infrastructure.

Each level in this system of concentric circles is somewhat insulated from the next, allowing for deniability at all stages. The preachers at the outer circle are not blowing themselves up, nor are they shooting anyone. They merely speak, incite, train, and preach under a religious umbrella, usually in places of worship. They are allowed to operate in all countries. Their activity is purely "spiritual"—atrocious, but "spiritual." It is designed to gain the silent support of the vast majority of Muslims, who would never support a suicide murder but would never oppose a religious leader. Their other role is to direct the orientation of the outer circle inward, not outward, condoning the terror and not joining the world in rejecting it.

The second circle resides safely in terrorist states, protected by the local governments, beyond the reach of any law. These are the whole-sale terror vendors. The vast majority of terror incidents are planned and commissioned in places like Iran, Syria, Lebanon, the Palestinian Authority, and—at least in the past—in Afghanistan and Iraq. The role of Yemen, Sudan, Somalia, and the allegedly reformed Libya is less than clear. Residency in such countries, and protection by their governments, guarantees freedom of terror. Yet these host countries are nevertheless respectable members of the United Nations, its Security Council, and its Human Rights Commission. They also have diplomatic and business relations with most of the Western world, elements of which are blind, greedy, or both.

Much like a multinational company, the terror conglomerates spread wholly owned subsidiaries and partly owned smaller outfits all over the globe, often under names that are unrecognizable and always changing. They keep lists of nonexistent organizations, whose names can be used in case deniability is necessary. Some of the subsidiaries have semi-independent CEOs, who conduct their own local murder business under loose supervision and strong financial support of the parent conglomerate. The second circle leans heavily on the moral and political support of the outer circle, sometimes obeying its general operational instructions, but often without any specific action orders.

Finally, the inner circle of the terrorists themselves is disposable. At the retail level, some blow themselves up, or get killed or caught; sometimes they even get away with their crimes. But no one really cares about them, least of all those who send them. In cases where they are caught, of course, they are protected by the selective civil liberties of the host country. They are never executed. If they receive long jail sentences, this invites kidnapping and hijacking to free them, more as an excuse for additional terror than out of a real desire to save the convicts. They cannot reveal too much about those who financed, armed, and sent them because they do not always know them, and anyone who tries to force them to speak is easily accused of violating their human rights.

Thus every single aspect of the free democratic system is ingeniously exploited by the terror network: free speech, freedom of religion, immunity of places of worship, free international travel, asylum to political refugees, foreign student fellowships, philanthropic attitudes, free flow of funds, freedom of publishing and broadcasting, the presumption of innocence, the right to remain silent, all other human rights—and, finally, the tendency of democracies to yield to blackmail under public pressure.

Even globalization, often viewed as a tool of rich nations and multinational companies eager to control the world, is successfully used by the terror networks. They are all over the Internet, they use and sometimes control satellite TV channels, their fund-raising is global, and the map of their atrocities covers all continents. They move money from one corner of the world to another, using endless covers such as religious organizations and welfare programs, claiming invasion of privacy and religious persecution, whenever caught. They are aware of the fact that the antiglobalization movement is fully global. They even fund major international gatherings against globalization, such as the recent conference in Beirut, sponsored by Hizbullah and several other terror organizations, hosting "peace activists" and other noble justice seekers.

As one banner carried in a street demonstration said: "Join the worldwide struggle against globalization."

— 4 —

THE VIRGINS ARE READY

Dear God: If you exist, don't let them use your name when performing atrocities. If you do not exist, please let them know it immediately.

A woman walks into an Israeli restaurant in Haifa at lunchtime. It is Saturday, a day of rest, when families enjoy quality time together. She sits alone, orders food, eats, observes families with old people and little children eating their lunch at nearby tables, laughing and chatting. She finishes her meal, and pays the bill—don't ask me why. She then blows herself up, killing twenty-one people, including many children, whose body fragments are scattered all around the restaurant. Many additional victims remain disabled for life, with pieces of metal in their heads and bodies. Entire families perish. She is called a "martyr" by several Arab leaders and an "activist" by the European press. Palestinian dignitaries condemn the act in public, but in private they visit her bereaved family, pay their respects, and also pay a generous financial reward.

This is not the worst suicide story to emerge in the past few years. There was also the man who walked into the festive Passover night

Seder meal in an Israeli hotel, attended mostly by old people, many of whom were Holocaust survivors. He stood in the middle of the dining room, had enough time to observe his intended victims, and then blew himself up, killing twenty-seven people, twenty-one of them over the age of seventy. Today he is a hero, his photo posted in numerous Palestinian schools and offices.

The Palestinian suicide murderers succeed in their avowed goal of killing Jews almost exclusively. Here the madness is at least consistent. But in Iraq many suicide murders kill only or mostly Iraqis, sometimes killing as many as twenty Iraqis with the hope that an American or two will die in the process. Even within the twisted logic and barbarian attitude of those who finance, arm, and dispatch suicide murderers, the wholesale killing of your own countrymen for the sake of murdering perhaps one or two foreigners is incomprehensible. But human evil knows no boundaries, as even Europe has demonstrated.

Suicide murders are not a new invention, but they have been made popular, if I may use the expression, only recently. Even after September 11, it seems that most of the Western world does not yet understand this very potent psychological weapon. Its real direct impact is relatively minor. The total number of casualties from hundreds of suicide murders within Israel in the last four years is about a fifth of those due to car accidents. September 11 was quantitatively much less lethal than many earthquakes. More people die from AIDS in one day in Africa than all the Russians who died in the hands of Chechnya-based Muslim suicide murderers since that conflict started. Each year, Saddam killed more people than all those who died from suicide murders since the Coalition occupation of Iraq.

So what is all the fuss about suicide killings? They create headlines. They are spectacular and frightening. Suicide bombing makes for a very cruel death, dismembering dozens of bystanders and inflicting horrible and severe lifelong injuries on those who survive. And it is always shown on television in great detail. One such murder, with the help of hysterical media coverage, can destroy the tourism industry of a country for quite a while, as it did in Bali and in Turkey.

But the real fear comes from the undisputed fact that no defense and no preventive measures can succeed against a determined suicide murderer. This has not yet penetrated the thinking of the Western world. The United States and Europe are constantly improving their defenses against the last murder, not the next one. We may arrange for the best airport security in the world, but if you want to commit murder by suicide, you don't have to board a plane to explode yourself and kill many people. Who could stop a suicide murder in the midst of the crowded line waiting to be checked by the airport metal detector? How about the lines to the check-in counters in a busy travel period? Put a metal detector in front of every train station in Spain, and the terrorists will target the buses. Protect the buses, and they will go after the movie theaters, concert halls, supermarkets, shopping malls, schools, and hospitals. Put guards in front of every concert hall, and the murderers will aim for the lines of people, killing both the attendees and the guards themselves. Preventive measures and strict border controls can help the problem, but they cannot eliminate it entirely. This war cannot be won in a defensive way.

What is behind the suicide murders? Money, power, and cold-blooded murderous incitement, nothing else. It has nothing to do with fanatical religious beliefs. No Muslim preacher has ever blown himself up, nor has any son of an Arab politician or religious leader. Wouldn't you expect some of the religious leaders to do it themselves, or to talk their sons into doing it, if this were truly a supreme act of religious fervor? Aren't they interested in the benefits of going to heaven? Instead they send outcast women, naive children, retarded people, and young hotheads. They promise them the delights — mostly sexual — of the next world, and pay their families handsomely after the supreme act is performed and enough innocent people are dead.

Suicide killing also has nothing to do with poverty and despair. The poorest region in the world, by far, is Africa, and suicide murder never happens there. There are countless desperate people in the world, in every culture, country, and continent. Desperation does not provide anyone with explosives, reconnaissance, and transportation.

There was certainly more despair in Saddam's Iraq than in Paul Bremer's, and no one exploded him or herself. A suicide murder is simply the weapon of cruel, inhuman, cynical, well-funded terrorists, who have no regard for human life, including the lives of their fellow countrymen, but have very high regard for their own affluent well-being and their hunger for power.

Some enlightened scholars and peace-loving people around the world have tried to understand the real motives of the individual suicide murderer. The subject has rightfully become the subject of psychological profiling and sophisticated analysis by social scientists. One problem is that when you spot a suicide murderer with an explosive belt, there's not much time to ask him to fill out a questionnaire about his or her motives, family history, and religious beliefs. There are only two choices: stop the suicide murderer or die, in which case you'll have little chance to analyze his or her answers. Yet these details have not been well understood in the halls of Western academia.

Only rarely do such figures live to explain themselves. One who did was a sixteen-year-old Palestinian—a shorter-than-average boy who looked thirteen and was always ridiculed by his friends. He believed that becoming a suicide murderer would make him a worshipped hero, and he "knew" that it would guarantee him the chance to be with seventy-two virgins, who are guaranteed in heaven to those who kill Jews. Needless to say, he could have accomplished nothing if not for the good people who provided him with an explosive belt, laced with nails and metal fragments, and sent him to blow himself up. Luckily he was stopped by Israeli soldiers on his way to explode and was saved, removing his suicide belt carefully in front of the CNN cameras before sharing his story.

In a different case, one woman in Gaza was caught by her husband having an affair with another man. Realizing that she was facing death at the hands of her husband, she was talked into exploding herself, killing a few Israelis in the process. Her lover provided the explosive belt, and her husband drove her to the place where she blew herself up. Some might call this the Jihad version of ménage à trois, but it is not funny at all. Imagine the tragedy of this woman! On hearing such stories, it's impossible not to wonder whether these are real human beings, whether this is the twenty-first century, and whether you're awake at all. The unfortunate answer to all three questions is yes.

The only way to fight the newly popular weapon of suicide is the same way one fights organized crime or pirates on the high seas: through offensive measures. As with organized crime, it is crucial that the forces on the offense be united, and that they take the battle all the way the top of the crime pyramid. Organized crime cannot be eliminated by arresting the little drug dealer on the street corner. It can only be brought down by going after the head of "the Family."

As long as part of the public supports it, and others tolerate it, trying to explain it away in terms of poverty or miserable childhood experiences, organized crime will thrive. So will terrorism. After September 11, the United States seems to understand this. Russia is beginning to understand it. Turkey understands it. I am very much afraid that most of Europe still does not understand it, and that this will not change until suicide murder arrives in Europe. In my humble opinion, this will definitely happen. The Spanish trains and the Istanbul bombings are only the beginning. The unity of the civilized world in fighting this horror is absolutely indispensable. Until Europe wakes up, this unity will not be achieved.

— 5 —

A TICKING BOMB

The fact that the terrorists force us to choose between dying and abandoning civil liberties is, by itself, a menace to our society.

.

It is high noon on a hot summer day in Israel. Parents come to a kindergarten to collect their children after school. An armed security guard is watching the scene. An Arabic-looking young man wearing a heavy topcoat—in the hot weather—approaches the parents and their children. No one else in sight is wearing more than a T-shirt. Under these circumstances, a heavy coat is likely to conceal an explosive suicide belt. Why would anyone wear such a coat on a hot summer day in Israel? A dozen children and their mothers are in immediate danger of horrible death. But the guard has no absolute proof that there is a suicide belt. Perhaps the young man is sick, mentally or otherwise. There could be any number of other explanations, although most would be far-fetched. What should the guard do? Kill the man instantly? Interrogate him, knowing that at any time he might pull the cord and explode, taking with him children, parents, and the guard?

A Palestinian driver is caught leaving Israeli territory into the Palestinian area. An antiterror listening post learns from his cell phone conversations that he has just delivered a suicide murderer with an explosive belt to an Israeli population center. Under police interrogation, at the place of arrest, he refuses to say where he left the murderer. Meanwhile, the murderer is likely to detonate his device within an hour, killing dozens of bus passengers or supermarket shoppers. You could probably get the information out of the driver through brute force, preventing the mass murder of innocent people. Would you? Should you? Do you have time to consult someone? Is there time for a symposium concerning the legal situation?

As I write these words, they might sound like a theoretical exercise in ethics or law. But in truth it is a real-life situation, one that happens frequently in numerous iterations, of varying severity and danger.

You stand there, in the hot daylight, a twenty-five-year-old guard, perhaps with a high school education, perhaps less. You see the cheerful children. You are sure that the man with the coat will kill them. The only way to stop him is to kill him instantly—kill, not wound, for merely wounding him might not prevent him from triggering his device. But you have no proof. Kill him, you worry, and you might be accused of murder. More likely, you will become a hero and save the children. One minute from now, you will know which one it is. Just imagine the situation. In the moments you have left, do you ponder the law, human rights, the values of our shared civilization? Do you shoot and kill, or do you hold your fire?

What if you're that policeman interrogating the driver. Do you use force? Do you beat him to get the information? Are you sure you will succeed? Do you have an alternative?

On the one hand, in both cases, the law states that you should not rush to judgment. On the other hand, common sense says that in both cases you should act, and act fast. But if you do choose to act—and then, perhaps, act again later, under slightly less ominous circumstances—before you know it you've begun to erode the foundation of our civilized society. The problem is that the person who has to make the decision is not a professor of ethics. He is not a justice of the Supreme Court. He is a young man, faced with an instant decision that may determine whether many people will die. But he is also determining whether civil liberties and human rights are the next victims of terror.

While indulging in this moral discussion, it's also important to remember the element of luck. Perhaps the man with the coat is indeed a suicide murderer, but the explosive belt is faulty and will not function. Perhaps he is an ultraorthodox Jew who wears a black coat even in the summer, but who has lost his black hat. Should he be killed because of the possibility that he might be a suicide bomber?

The situation is paradoxical. In a bipolar world with civilization and terror as the two poles, terrorists exploit every aspect of civilization in order to destroy it. Sometimes it seems that the only way for us to fight terror is to perform uncivilized acts to defend civilization.

Thus we've arrived at the junction where a scientist might follow logic, but the proverbial taxi driver would prefer common sense.

None of this should be painted in black or white. It is absolutely clear that if we insist on preserving, in all cases and in all situations, democracy, human rights, civil liberties, and the rule of law, we will hand the terrorists and their sponsors an irreversible global victory. It is equally clear that, if we completely abandon these values in order to beat terror, we will have lost the very thing for which we are willing to fight. The lesson is loud and clear: Pure black and pure white each guarantee defeat. Where logic ends, common sense must take over.

If you want to be philosophical about it, the fact that the terrorists have forced us to face such dilemmas is as great a threat to our society as the murders themselves. The only difference, perhaps, is that we can always change our minds about our civil liberties—but the death of the victims cannot be reversed.

There is another paradox here. To win the war against the terror networks, it is necessary to prevent terror attacks and to eliminate the terrorists. When the war succeeds, it becomes invisible and the public begins to suspect, mistakenly, that it does not exist. On September 12, 2001, the day after the terrorist attacks in New York and the Pentagon, most Americans were willing to suspend some of their civil liberties to fight terror. A couple of years later, understandably, the pendulum has swung the other way. This is a strange, self-regulating war. The more you win, the more you limit yourself. But when you are defeated, you allow yourself to use additional tools. Suspending certain liberties and human rights is, definitely, a tool of questionable virtue. However, it may be indispensable. Who is to decide?

Courts in several countries—especially the Israeli Supreme Court, which has long been "suspected" of being very liberal—have debated such issues endlessly. They weigh the black and white, and almost always answer in shades of gray. I do not pretend to know the answers. In a very personal way, I hope I will never face such a dilemma. But if I am honest with myself, I must admit that I would probably err in the direction of safety—that I would stop that young man in the heavy topcoat. And I'd bet that the leaders of the American Civil Liberties Union, Amnesty International, and other organizations would do the same, even if they might deny it in the abstract. This is a very sad conclusion, but sometimes it is sad to be human.

— 6 —

REWRITING
INTERNATIONAL LAW

Dealing with suicide murderers and with their dispatchers by current international law is like filing a malpractice suit against a poisonous snake.

It is likely that when humanity finally settles outer space, international law will have to be changed substantially. New situations, new violations, and new rules will be abundant. Everything will have to be reexamined. The law books will have to be thoroughly rewritten. In fact, the best evidence that intelligent creatures do exist in outer space is the fact that they do not try to communicate with us or to use our laws.

Global terrorism is different from anything we have ever seen, just as life in space will be different from anything we do here on Earth. Every major war in history has led to modifications of what has been internationally recognized as legal or illegal, accepted or unaccepted behavior. I firmly believe that the current world conflict will rewrite numerous aspects of international law. The sooner it happens, the better off the world will be.

I have listed earlier some of the fields in which I am not a professional, including history, journalism, politics, and Middle Eastern affairs. In the interest of full disclosure I should add that I am not a lawyer or a jurist, either. My father, Izhar, was an attorney and a politician. His name has an interesting history. His father, Haim Harari, was the last of my ancestors to arrive in Israel, in 1897. A Hebrew language teacher, he knew that the biblical names Isaac, Jacob, and Joseph were actually Hebrew verbs: Isaac means "he will laugh," Jacob means "he will follow," and Joseph means "he will add." The Book of Genesis explains the background. When his son was born, he invented a brand-new Hebrew name, Izhar, meaning "he will shine." In the best biblical tradition, it was another name that began as a verb.

My father, Izhar, was a member of the Israeli Parliament (the Knesset) for its first twenty-five years. He wrote its first rules of procedure and authored the bill outlining the method by which Israel would build its constitution step by step. I learned from him that the law should reflect reality and must evolve with events. The law is a living thing; new situations require new or revised laws. The proverbial taxi driver in me believes that common sense must play a crucial role in adapting any decent system of justice to real life.

The world war we are witnessing today covers numerous countries, but it was never declared by anyone. It is not even clear who the sides are—who is at war with whom. One side has no army, no uniforms, no address, and no law of any kind. It does not always have a name. Actually, it often has too many different names. It is accountable to no one. From this point of view, it has the legal characteristics of criminals or organized crime. But it claims to have national, or even regional or global, aspirations, and it is protected by sovereign governments, who do not admit it. It honors no rules whatsoever—whereas even the Nazis, whose horrors have never been matched and hopefully never will, did obey certain rules.

After the carnage of World War II, it became unacceptable to bomb population centers with no military or strategic targets in the area. It is definitely unacceptable to kill innocent civilians deliberately. But in the current war, one side—the terrorists—kills civilians almost exclusively, and is almost entirely made up of civilians itself. Their declared goal is to wipe out entire countries and bring modern civilization to an end. Fighting them means searching and hitting only civilians, although a very specific kind of civilians. They are certainly not identifiable by uniforms or by any other internationally accepted military attribute. They cannot even be defined as "armed civilians." Leaving their weapons at home does not make them righteous. They cannot be dealt with by police action. Normal international order requires that police deal with civilian criminals and armies deal with opposing armies. Here armies must be used to fight civilian murderers, whether they are called criminals, terrorists, or "fighters."

Even in such benign, abstract terms, we already face a severe media problem. When a leading murderer and his active associates are eliminated, the media may truthfully announce that "civilians were killed," turning a true victory over evil into an alleged crime. It requires a certain mixture of stupidity, bias, or both to make such a claim, but the practice is common.

If you accept that such "civilians" cannot be the targets of military action, however, you grant them absolute immunity. Armies cannot touch them because they are civilians. Police from the defending country cannot operate on foreign soil. The host government takes no measures against its resident terrorists. In fact, it nurtures them, while permanently denying it. Does it follow that international law guarantees immunity to such people, regardless of any atrocities they may perform?

Are terrorists considered soldiers or civilians? When they are killed, they are claimed to be "innocent civilians." When they are caught they invoke the Geneva Convention, as if they were prisoners of war, not criminals. Therefore, they claim, they cannot be brought to trial. International law knows how to deal with soldiers fighting a war or with civilian criminals—but not yet with people who oscillate between the two definitions at their convenience.

When such people intentionally and deliberately murder children and elderly people, they are "fighting for national liberation." When their leaders proudly claim responsibility for such acts, it is accepted as a part of the game. But when a real innocent civilian in their neighborhood is accidentally hurt, during an attack on the terrorists, it is allegedly a "war crime."

Yet all of this is a matter of nomenclature and semantics. It only gets more complicated when we move into matters of action. Do you raid a mosque that serves as a terrorist ammunition storage facility? Do you storm a church in which terrorists have seized the priests as hostages? Do you return fire into the minaret of a mosque, if you are attacked from there? If you do, are you in violation of some sacred international legal principles, or are you acting in self-defense? What does international law says about these situations?

The questions continue: Do you return fire if you are attacked from a hospital or shot at from an ambulance? How do you deal with a terrorist command post located among the patients in a mental hospital? What do you do when a healthy multiple murderer escapes into a hospital ward and pretends to be a sick patient, with the active or passive support of the medical staff? And if you deal with these situations in the way I think you should, how would it look on the TV screens in living rooms five thousand miles away? There will always be a grim doctor available to describe—on camera, naturally—how the soldiers broke into his hospital. What does international law say about these situations?

What if you are facing a band of stone-throwing children, well guided by an unseen adult director? Obviously you don't shoot. There are other police means for dispersing such demonstrations. But what if, behind the children, there are armed adults, shooting at you and being protected by the human shield of the rioting children? Do you just remain defenseless? Do you shoot back? Do you die, just to leave a good impression somewhere? Television cameras are aimed at you, showing you and the rioting children but not the shooting adults. What solutions can international law offer in such circumstances?

In fact, how do you react to people who cowardly recruit children for war and deliberately send them to die? We have seen this in the

Iran-Iraq war, and we now see it in the Palestinian areas. Hitler also drafted sixteen-year-olds at the end of World War II, but he dressed them in uniforms and did not pretend that they were civilians. Today children are used as human shields daily and are often sent out as suicide murderers. Some of the most senior terror ringleaders are surrounded by children constantly as they move from place to place, knowing that this protects them. What does international law have to say about that?

Such situations are new, unprecedented in human history. They are the products of the dirtiest war ever fought, including the two world wars. There is no dirty trick the terrorists have not attempted. But their ultimate weapon, which has gone unremarked upon by international law and by the international community, is the phalanx of countries that provide safe havens to the ringleaders.

Imagine a purely hypothetical situation in which the leadership of the IRA resides in a well-known address in Dublin, enjoying VIP hospitality, while it guides and commands terrorist attacks in London, Belfast, and elsewhere, openly claiming responsibility for these attacks and declaring them to be a war of liberation. Hundreds of men, women, and children are killed in the streets, buses, supermarkets, and shopping malls. At the same time, the perpetrators meet regularly with ministers and officials of the Irish government, who know who they are, where they are, and what they are doing. They also participate in public functions, receptions, and social events, and enjoy the protection of their host government. And yet the Irish government declares that it knows nothing about them, or that they do not exist at all, or that it is too weak to control them, or that their acts are purely political, or all of the above. Would an attack on Ireland be justified by international law, or would that law allow them to continue with their murders indefinitely? I know how the British government would address such a situation in Ireland. When it comes to Israel, its approach might be somewhat different.

The problem is that the civilized world is still having illusions about the rule of law in a totally lawless environment. It is trying to play ice hockey with a team of figure skaters, sending a chess champion to knock out a heavyweight boxer. Just as no country has a law forbidding cannibals from eating their prime minister, because such an act is unthinkable, international law has no special penalties to cover killers shooting from hospitals, mosques, and schools while being protected by their government or society. International law does not know how to handle someone who uses children as human shields, while being sheltered by a government. International law does not know how to deal with a leader of murderers who is royally and comfortably hosted by a country that pretends to condemn his acts or just claims to be too weak to arrest him. And yet, amazingly, many such "heroes" demand protection under international law and define all those who attack them as war criminals—and some Western media are all to happy to repeat the allegations.

The good news is that all of this is temporary because the evolution of international law has always adapted itself to reality. The punishment for suicide murder should be death or arrest *before* the murder, not during or after. After every world war, the rules of international law have changed; the same will happen after this one. In the darkness before the dawn, however, significant harm can be done.

At this point, you might be pausing to ponder the disturbing prospects I've laid before you. "But what about our international organizations?" I hear you say. "The United Nations? The International Red Cross? The International Court of Justice? The UN Human Rights Commission. They must be the solution."

You must be kidding.

— 7 —

THE REFEREE IS BIASED

The jury is out. It better not come back.

O nce upon a time, there was a large distant country named Globania. It pretended to be a democracy with a fair judicial system, human rights organizations, and a social welfare system. It had a parliament of 191 members. Yet an absolute majority of these members did not believe in democracy and had never lived in one. Many of them believed that women are inferior and do not deserve the protection of law. Some of the judges in the highest court of Globania came from districts in which there was no independent judicial system and no rule of law. They were appointed by the politicians in the parliament, most of whom would not have recognized a fair system of justice if they saw one up close. The chair of the human rights commission, another official elected by the parliament, was one of the worst violators of human rights in the land. In Globania, there was also a tiny ethnic minority, represented in parliament by only one member. This minority was intensely despised by the nondemocratic majority in the parliament, some of whose members demanded the physical extinction of this minority, openly and without reprimand.

Whenever someone from this minority was murdered for racist reasons, neither the parliament nor the courts ever reacted or brought the murderer to justice. None of the social welfare services were available to this minority.

Would you like to have lived in Globania as an ordinary citizen? Would you like to have been a member of this tiny minority? Would you consider the "democratic" decisions of this parliament acceptable? Could you defend the rulings of its high court?

Does it bother you that Globania is your home planet?

The United Nations has 191 members. Most of them are not democratic countries and have dubious judicial systems. Only one of them has been threatened with total physical extinction by other member states, as the other members watched without reacting. Only one of them has had its Olympic athletes murdered, with no resolutions passed to condemn the act. But the organization responsible for murdering the athletes is the only entity, which is neither a state nor an international organization, that has been invited as a permanent observer to the United Nations. Only one member state cannot be elected to any important committee of the United Nations and was not allowed to belong to any geographical region or group of states. Only one nation of refugees has never been helped by the UN high commissioner on refugees. Only one member has a capital city unrecognized by the organization and by most of its members. Only one member state has watched as its sworn enemy addressed the UN General Assembly, armed with a pistol, even though he was not a head of state.

If you have guessed that this member state is Israel—and if you remember that Libya was until recently the chair of the UN Human Rights Commission, and that Algeria is a member of its security council—you are beginning to understand the situation. If you can remember one UN General Assembly condemnation of an Arab attack on Israel, whether a total war or a particularly ugly terrorist attack, in the past fifty-seven years, your memory is playing tricks on you. There has never been such a condemnation. Not for plane hijacking, not for the Olympic murders, not for suicide murders, not for a deliberate massacre of children in a school bus, not for taking school kids as hostages, not for blowing up passenger airplanes, not for shelling towns and villages, not for attacking embassies, synagogues, and Jewish institutions abroad, not for blocking commercial shipping, and not for attacking passengers in airports before or after their flight. So much for the integrity of international organizations that deal with terror and international law.

Is Israel an absolutely righteous country that never does wrong and never errs? Of course not. Like Belgium, Israel has a significant Arab minority, whose levels of education and income are well below the rest of the population. Like France and the Netherlands—although somewhat less so—Israel has its share of extreme right-wing political forces. Like Britain, Israel believes it should defend itself against terror. Unlike Britain, it does so in the neighborhood, not in the Malvinas and Iraq. Like Finland, it has a record number of cell phones. Like Austria, it has a dominant religion, but complete religious freedom. Like the United States, it has a huge number of high-tech start-up companies. Like Spain, it has a large, but not dominant, percentage of religiously devout citizens. Like Singapore, it is surrounded by hundreds of millions of Muslims. Like Italy, it has ugly cases of political corruption. Like Switzerland, it has separate school systems for people who prefer to learn in different languages. Like Japan, it has one of the highest life expectancies in the world. Like Canada, it is a melting pot of people from many cultures. Like Sweden, it has high-quality scientific research. Like all of the above, it is a democracy. Like none of the above, it is permanently threatened by extinction.

No one criticizes the Israeli government more often than the Israelis, and they know that there is much to change and improve. Israeli democracy is rather wild, and the Israeli press habitually crosses the reasonable boundaries of free speech. But this is all done within the framework of normal political criticism, within a democratic system, augmented by the Jewish tradition of overdoing everything. The Israeli analogue of the *New York Times* or *Le Monde* is the daily *Ha'aretz*. It is often said that the last time it supported the government was during the British Mandate before 1948.

As an Israeli citizen, I personally object to more decisions made by my government than you ever want to hear about, and I have voted against a reigning government more often than I have voted in its favor. I see no reason to establish Jewish villages in the middle of densely populated Arab areas. I know that some young Israeli soldiers have been more trigger-happy than they should have. I also know that—in one and only one case—a horrible mass murder of innocent praying Muslims was performed in Hebron by an Israeli terrorist who died on the scene. We will discuss Israel, its problems, achievements, and misdeeds later. But to use a polite understatement, the obsession of so many international organizations with condemning Israel, rather than defending it, is a loud and clear reason to doubt their impartiality.

Consider the relatively benign case of the International Red Cross. The cross is a Christian religious symbol. It is not surprising that other religions prefer their first aid services to be symbolized by other signs. The International Red Cross respects this wish and allows other approved symbols to be used in specific countries, where they are internationally recognized as equivalent to the Red Cross. Naturally, the Red Crescent, used all over the Arab world, is one such symbol. There is only one country whose symbol has not been approved: Israel's Star of David. This was the ruling of the automatic, nondemocratic majority, despite years of appeals to change the ruling. This may seem a minor, secondary issue, but it offers glaring proof that the referee is biased. The counterarguments are all easily disproved. Is it because the emblem of one single country should not be recognized? The Red Lion, the symbol of Iran, was approved long ago. Is it because Muslims would be filled with anger by the sight of a Red Star of David and refuse to respect the immunity of the symbol? Israeli ambulances are, of course, marked by a Red Star of David, so this argument is ridiculous. There is only one reason: The nondemocratic majority of Globania does not like the Star of David.

An interesting case is the recent ruling of the International Court of Justice concerning the fence, or wall or barrier, being built by Israel as a defense against suicide murderers. Can anyone explain why the Israeli settlements in the West Bank were never referred to this court, even though some of them existed for thirty-seven years, while the brand new wall, certainly less permanent and less threatening, was immediately dispatched to this court? The proverbial taxi driver in me has a very good guess: The settlements, as infuriating as they are to the Palestinians, cannot prevent suicide murders. The fence or wall does, and it has been proven to work. Obviously this is unacceptable. The more I think about it, the more I am convinced that there cannot be another reason.

Stupidly, the Israeli government designed the wall to go through all sorts of unnecessary places, causing unjustified problems and injustice in many areas. The Israeli Supreme Court, whose independence and courage are disliked by some people in Israel, has overruled many of these geographic details in the interest of Palestinians residing nearby. But the Israeli court does recognize Israel's (or anyone else's) right to defend itself against suicide murders, while the International Court of Justice thinks nothing of the sort. After all, its appointing body, the United Nations, has never stated that suicide murders in Israel are really a bad thing.

The idea that self-defense is a sacred right only against attacking sovereign states, and not against terrorists and terror organizations, is a true miracle of "justice," applied by the Globanian Court of Justice to one defending country. Before the case was considered, nearly every democracy in the world announced that this court had no jurisdiction on such a political dispute. But the democracies are a small minority in Globania, and the International Court of Justice, including its two Arab judges, must please those who have appointed it. And once the court has ruled, how could anyone dare to challenge it?

Actually, on all matters related to Israel, Globania has a jury system, in which one side of the dispute selects the jury and the other side pays the price. Is it even remotely thinkable that one of the judges might come from Israel? Would it ever occur to an Arab judge to disqualify himself from participating in such matters? Perhaps in Albania. Certainly not in Globania.

In recent years, UN-sponsored conferences—whatever their topic—have increasingly become staging areas for further attacks on Israel. In conferences on women's issues, the majority, consisting of totalitarian countries in which women are second-class citizens at best, have found excuses to pass anti-Israeli resolutions. The international union of parliaments, many of which are a mockery, has also had much to say about the Israeli parliament—which, whatever its faults, is at least a true democracy. Those who send children to commit suicide murders and use them repeatedly as human shields, pass anti-Israeli resolutions in international conferences on children's issues. And so it goes, on and on.

PART II

THE HESITANT
WORLD

~ 8 ~

TROUBLE IN GLOBANIA

Globalization plus democracy equals the end of democracy.

Countless citizens of Globania have never seen a telephone, cellular or otherwise. Many of them have never attended school or have attended elementary school at best. There are hundreds of millions of Globanians who never drink clean water and have no medical care. Yet in other parts of Globania not only is the water clean, but there are also many more telephones than people, university education is free and abundant, and MRI tests and elective plastic surgery are available to those who need or want them. The gap between rich and poor in Globania is incomprehensible, and it shows not the slightest sign of diminishing.

Two generations ago, at a time when natural resources were the most valuable economic commodities, oil was discovered in some of the poorest areas of Globania. It looked like progress might finally catch up, at least in the oil-rich areas. That opportunity was totally wasted by the owners of the newly discovered wealth, who chose not to use it to further the major educational, social, and cultural changes that were needed in the region. Some of these owners were the rulers of the poor areas; others were the owners of large Globanian companies, representing other interests. Neither of these groups has embarked on serious initiatives for educating the people. One might argue that the symbolic pinnacle of this attitude was Saddam Hussein's financial support of families of Palestinian suicide murderers, using the funds obtained from the United Nations' Oil for Food program.

While this was happening, a new revolution began. It goes by several names—the Electronic Revolution, the Information Age, the Postindustrial Era—all somewhat obscure and most conveying a mixture of awe, excitement, and suspicion. The main characteristic of this revolution is the central economic role of knowledge, know-how, science, technology, and intellectual property of various kinds. Their value exceeds that of even the most precious natural resources. More than ever, the gap between educated and uneducated has become a gap between rich and poor.

Most of the large oil-producing regions of the world have chosen not to participate in the knowledge revolution. They are a little less poor than they would have been without oil, but by most measures they still lag behind the rest of the world, and what wealth they have is concentrated in a few hands. Their per capita GDP is much lower than that of any advanced country. The only exceptions are the tiny oil-rich Gulf states, which are truly affluent, making them the preferred targets of "hostile takeover bids" by their large, aggressive neighbors and by the terrorists. Saddam's invasion of Kuwait may only be the pilot project of this trend.

More than ever, Globania is divided not so much between those who have and those who have not, but between those who are well-educated and those who are not. A rough estimate tells us that, of the six billion people on this planet, approximately one billion are full participants in the knowledge revolution in one way or another; another billion are trying with reasonable success to join in, and four billion are largely unaware that the revolution is taking place.

Unless this can be reversed, this means trouble—big trouble.

To this we must add a paradox, which may convert the big trouble into an irreversible disaster. The technology revolution created globalization. The ability to watch the human suffering in Sudan in a posh living room in New York or in Kuwait City is slowly turning Globania into one huge entity, the famous "global village." The ability to send messages, ideas, newscasts, money, manuscripts, pictures, and any other form of information in less than a second, from Seoul to Buenos Aires, is here. The ability to send representatives, soldiers, goods, and missiles, from anywhere to anywhere in hours, is also here.

The evidence of globalism is all around us. Recently, my Viennese wife and I were sipping our Italian espresso with a German Black Forest cake at the Stanford Shopping Center in California's Silicon Valley, when we heard the best-known Israeli song, "Hava Nagila," being played at the table behind us. It was coming from a Nokia cellular phone, made in Finland or, most likely, somewhere in Asia. The music stopped and the Japanese man holding the phone said: "Moshimoshi."

It was truly a global moment.

So we are all gradually becoming citizens of one large political entity, our beloved Globania. At the moment, a poor villager in China may not yet feel any kinship to a nomad in the Saudi desert or to a Wall Street tycoon. But a Polish farmer and a Sicilian policeman are already obeying the same European laws; Taiwanese workers are producing running shoes for New York executives; and when you call Lufthansa from Chicago, you may be connected to someone sitting in India. In an extremely slow but absolutely clear process, national boundaries are gradually disappearing.

As good citizens of our global country, we should be extremely concerned. It is bad enough that we have huge and growing gaps between rich and poor, educated and uneducated. But most of the affluent areas of Globania have zero or negative population growth, while the population of the poor areas—the ones without education, with little or no democracy, with contaminated water, minimal health systems, and no awareness of the knowledge revolution—is increasing rapidly. To make things worse, wherever religious fanaticism is the norm, fertility is even higher. The per capita GDP of many of these regions is declining, simply because the population increase outperforms the economic growth.

At the same time the per capita GDP of some of the affluent countries grows, not only because their economies are expanding but also because their population is stable or decreasing.

And where is the paradox? The only hope of educating the people from the areas and nations that still lag behind is with the help of the wealthier, educated parts of the world. We do not want this to happen through a rerun of the colonial period, in which the rich countries seize and exploit the poor ones. So it must happen through a gradual process of democratization and enlightenment, led by the educated nations, with full cooperation of the beneficiaries.

Yet today there is a clear antidemocratic majority in Globania. As you read these words, that majority is increasing by the moment. It is not at all clear how a world that is dominated more and more by uneducated, undemocratic forces can survive this process.

Actually, the situation is even worse than this quick sketch suggests. Poor countries with larger and larger populations are becoming less and less powerful and successful. This is a clear antidemocratic trend. The more people one represents, the less significant he or she becomes. Moreover, many of the rulers of such societies have an interest in preventing enlightenment from reaching their citizens. Knowledge and education are always a threat to a corrupt, fanatical dictator.

Imagine for a moment that we have reached complete globalization and the ultimate democracy. The entire planet is one political entity and that entity has a democratically elected government. Sound great? Not at all. If this were to happen here and now, the elected Globanian government would be ruled by an antidemocratic coalition. The governing absolute majority of this coalition would grow significantly from one election campaign to the next, simply because of the demographic patterns. At the same time, that majority will represent smaller and smaller economic interests. This is a clear formula for a disaster.

"This is a gross oversimplification," you say. "We're not there, and we won't be there any time soon." Perhaps, but that's where we're heading, slowly but surely. There may be attempts to slow it down, but all of them are doomed, unless the affluent parts of the world invest in education, education, and education in the poorer areas.

Restricting immigration and reducing access to travel are some of the proposed remedies of the Western world. They are currently practiced by the United States and the European Union, and they have always been practiced by Japan. This may be a helpful temporary antiterror device, but it is not a long-range remedy for the ills of Globania.

In the long run, the flow of the poor into the wealthier regions cannot be completely blocked. The affluent world needs the immigration as much as the immigrants need it. A society with an increasing average age, declining birth rates, declining workforce, and elaborate social systems simply cannot survive without an influx of a reasonably educated workforce of immigrants. But it is crucial that these immigrants merge (if not necessarily assimilate) with the population of the host societies. The success of immigrant countries, such as the United States and Canada, stems precisely from the creation of such a melting pot. Emigrating from Algeria to Belgium or from Turkey to Austria without ever having worn a veil and starting to wear a head scarf after arriving there is certainly not the right formula. A true melting pot can only be created if the immigrants are proud to be the citizens of their new country, not if they come to convert it to the practices of the culture from which they have escaped. Moving a religiously fanatical community from one location to another is certainly not an acceptable solution to the world's problems.

There is a very clear correlation between the education of parents and their children. I am not talking about talents or about genetics. I am simply referring to the obvious fact that well-educated parents will always do everything in their economic power to provide education for their children, while uneducated parents will not always do so at their own initiative—because they cannot afford it, or they're not interested, or both. If every educated couple has one child and every uneducated couple has five, the decline in education and the increase of the uneducated majority becomes disastrous.

Unless the rich and developed regions of Globania embark on a monumental effort to educate their poor brothers, the equation is simple: Globalization plus democracy equals the end of democracy. In the absence of an educational revolution, the nondemocratic, uneducated majority will dramatically increase from decade to decade. This can lead only to a disaster, the first signs of which are beginning to show. As in any country that harbors both the very rich and the very poor, the poor Globanians will move into the richer areas, the rich will try to block them, and the poor will turn to weapons such as illegal immigration, crime, and terror to achieve their goals.

Despite all this, one should not conclude that there is the slightest justification for world terrorism or the slightest need to go soft on it. Terror should be eliminated by all possible methods, involving any combination of offense and defense, and terrorists should be pursued by all means and with all available force and determination until they are totally annihilated. This should be done regardless of the long-range global educational crisis. At the same time, however, the attempts to remedy that crisis should proceed as though terror did not exist. The all-out war against terror is emergency surgery necessary to save the life of the patient. The long-run education effort is a process of rehabilitation and prevention.

Both are crucial.

— 9 —

INTELLECTUAL PROPERTY AND INTELLECTUAL POVERTY

A grain of science brings more profit than a barrel of oil.

The Bible tells us that Moses took the children of Israel out of Egypt and wandered in the desert for forty years until he found the only place in the Middle East in which there was no oil. But Moses was no fool. He must have known that, one day, at the end of the twentieth century, intellectual property would have a larger economic value than oil. He therefore did collect, on Mount Sinai, a piece of intellectual property—or, perhaps, software—known as the Ten Commandments. Somehow this acquisition has indirectly led to the fact that, even though Israel has no oil and no other natural resources, its per capita GDP is among the twenty-five highest in the world, ahead of all the large oil-producing countries in the region.

There is no greater indicator of the intellectual property revolution than the comparison between the economies of countries with knowledge but no natural resources, and those of oil-rich countries with very few intellectual property assets. Japan, Singapore, Finland, and Israel are four examples of the first kind. Iran, Saudi Arabia,

Libya, and Nigeria are four examples of the second. Israel is the poorest among the countries of the first quartet, and Saudi Arabia is by far the richest among the second group. Yet Israel's per capita GDP is approximately twice that of Saudi Arabia. Yes, you read that correctly: Israel, with all its problems, is on average twice as affluent as the rich Saudis.

How did that happen? Technology, science, and knowledge.

Incidentally, the economic story of the piece of intellectual property called monotheism is not a pretty one. The inventor did not apply for a patent. Today he has, worldwide, approximately 12 million customers, the largest communities being in Israel and the United States. Two other entrepreneurs, who modified the product in a relatively minor way, succeeded in marketing it to at least a billion people each. Christianity and Islam have large following. Judaism remains, quantitatively, a tiny religion, while the absence of a patent on monotheism implies that no royalties are being paid.

The raging technology revolution involves innumerable major breakthroughs based on mathematics, computer science, physics, electronics, and material science, all of which have changed our lives. The results of these efforts can be found on our desks, in our houses, in airplanes and airports, cars and trains, printed and electronic media, military equipment, movies, recorded music, and the whole of Internet-based commerce, to name just a few. If there is one familiar symbol of this revolution, it might be the plastic mouse you use to "steer" your computer—a familiar daily object that no one could have understood thirty years ago.

But information technology is not the only player. There is also a genetic revolution in the making, which may have an even greater impact on our life, our death, our health, our food, and the way we produce children. The Genome Project, stem cell research, genetically modified organisms, "designer drugs," and DNA tests are just a few of the relevant buzzwords. The genetic revolution is driven by biological research—mostly with mice although not the plastic ones mentioned above but live ones.

For those of us who live in the affluent regions, the first revolution is already in our pockets, in the form of cell phones and handheld computers, while the second revolution is still negotiating its way into our daily life. For those who live in the underprivileged areas, neither revolution exists. In fact, most of these people never heard of the revolutions and many of them do not even have pockets at all.

There is also an emerging, mind-boggling, marriage of the two revolutions, in the form of technologies that combine breakthroughs in the medical and biological sciences with the innovations of physics, electronics, and computer science. Computerized diagnostic medical equipment, connections between brain and computer, advanced digital genetic analysis, laser surgery, radiation therapy, modern forensics, and new drugs are just a few examples of this bizarre mating of the two kinds of mice, living and plastic.

We will not discuss here all the implications of these revolutions, but one fact is clear: As all of this moves ahead at a breathtaking speed, the poorer regions of our planet are falling further and further behind, producing more children, educating them less and less, and remaining hopelessly in the hands of those who exploit their lack of education.

The discoveries of science, and the technological products that follow, have no intrinsic positive or negative value. They are tools. Science is invaluable in the development of humanity, in curing diseases, creating new sources of energy and new types of food, allowing us to enjoy much better living conditions and bringing cultural treasures closer to us. Science helps us detect cancer in a CAT scan and terrorist weapons in an airport scan. Science and technology allow us to fly to the best museums and opera houses, to view art over the Internet, to listen to music on our MP3 player. Science can also be harmful in more ways than one, and it is definitely no substitute for human values, ideals, art, and plain happiness. Science can be one of the most exciting ways of advancing our knowledge and learning about the universe, about nature and about us. All of this has always been so. But now science and technology have become critical economic assets, and this is what makes them a mandatory part of twenty-first-century education.

Religious fanaticism is simply inconsistent with science. Religion can coexist with science; fanaticism cannot. Truth is a crucial ingredient of science. A society based on lies cannot advance in science. Superstitions are an antithesis of science.

Likewise, an educational revolution cannot exclude women. In a poor society, it must actually *start* with women, who hold the key to so many aspects of early education. The difficulty of revolutionizing education in a society is directly proportional to the number of children in such a society. At some point, the attention each child receives will be limited by sheer physical factors, as needs outstrip resources.

There are many poor nations in the world, and many poor communities within even affluent countries. But material poverty is one thing and intellectual poverty is another. One can be wealthy without intellectual property, like the Gulf states, or with it, like Sweden. Similarly, not all poor people have the same affinity for education, especially in the era of science and technology.

An impoverished society, in which women are repressed, fertility rates are very high, and incitement based on lies is common, can be defined as suffering from intellectual poverty. Not all poor societies answer to such a description. Unfortunately, the kind of Islam exported primarily by Saudi Arabia and Iran to the rest of the Muslim world can be diagnosed as having all of these attributes. This has been repeatedly argued by serious Muslim scholars, who believe that this state of affairs is not at all based on the true values of Islam and is disastrous for the hundreds of millions of Muslims who are sentenced to intellectual—and therefore material—poverty as a result.

This can only bring catastrophe—first and foremost to the Islamic countries, although en route the rest of the world will have to pay a dear price. It is not too late to reverse the trend, but this can only be done by a generation of determined, antiterror, pro-education, pro-women, Muslim leaders.

Am I naive to dream about such leaders? Perhaps. But twenty-five years ago no one was dreaming of cell phones, plastic mice, September 11, or the genetic revolution.

—10—

THERE GOES THE
NEIGHBORHOOD

*The biblical Abraham, father of the Arabs and the Jews, offered
his wife to the king, tried to sacrifice his son, and sent his mis-
tress and his other son to the desert. So what do you expect?*

We have already reprimanded Moses for choosing the oil-free
land for his people. It is a tiny piece of land, at the crossroads
of Europe, Asia, and Africa. Throughout history, anyone who
wanted to conquer anything in the neighborhood had to control it. Israel is as big as New Jersey and smaller than Albania, but it cannot
sneeze without getting into the headline news all around the world.
More than once I have opened a European paper and found an incident with a few casualties in Israel on page one, while a much bigger
catastrophe elsewhere was relegated to page seven. Why? It's an interesting question.

This widespread media coverage is not new. When the children of
Israel were crossing the Sinai desert, Moses was informed that the
Egyptians were pursuing them. "What shall we do?" he asked his science and technology adviser. The latter proposed a major engineering
project: drying a passage through the red sea, crossing it, and covering

it back with water to block the Egyptians. "How long will it take?" Moses asked. "Several months," was the quick answer. Moses turned to his public relations adviser and said, "They are going to reach us tomorrow. What shall we do?" The media expert proposed: "Raise your hands. The water will split. We will cross. Lower your hands. The water will come back. The Egyptians will drown." "Do you really think this will work?" asked the skeptical leader. "I don't know. But if it will, I will get you a full page in the Bible."

One way or another, this was never a boring neighborhood. The land, which connects three continents, has been conquered by just about everybody, at one time or another: Israelites, Egyptians, Assyrians, Babylonians, Persians, Greeks, Romans, Arabs, Crusaders, Turks, and the British, to name just a few entries in the glorious list of the past three thousand years. Most of them declared it to be sacred to their religions. In centuries of Muslim conquest, it was always part of something else, usually a Syrian province.

"There goes the neighborhood," says the proverbial American homeowner when a minority family moves into the next house. It does not matter whether the newcomers are better educated, more affluent, or better behaved than their neighbors. The Arabs, apparently, feel much the same way about Israel. Bringing advanced agriculture, modern medicine, first-class science, and cutting-edge technology create only envy, not pride—and there goes the neighborhood.

A satellite photograph of the Middle East shows clearly the different colors of the land of pre-1967 Israel and its Arab neighbors, including the West Bank. The former border is easily visible; Israel is predominantly green, reflecting thriving agriculture, while the neighboring areas are all brown, indicating bare hills and desert. And in case you suspect that this reflects a different availability of water or better soil, just look at the narrow corridor between Tel Aviv and Jerusalem, which was always in Israeli hands, and compare it to the areas to the north and south, which were in Arab hands until 1967 and remain under the Palestinian Authority today. Same land, same soil, same water conditions. Green versus brown, and dramatically enough that one can see the difference from outer space.

But let us look at the entire neighborhood. First, the next-door neighbors: Egypt, Syria, Lebanon, and Jordan. Each of these nations has fought Israel several times, but now Egypt and Jordan have peace agreements with Israel, and I will risk the prediction that one day peace will be reached with the two others. For years, at the height of the U.S.-Soviet Cold War, I puzzled my American friends by saying that I hoped Israel and the Arabs would one day reach the same stage of relations as the hostile big powers. "Is this tense coexistence something to look forward to?" they asked. I pointed out that, during the entire Cold War period, each superpower had an ambassador in the other capital; travel, although limited, was allowed between the two countries; the countries recognized each other's existence; and they were always willing to talk to each other. If we could only get the Egyptians and the others to this stage, I argued, it would be wonderful. Today, thanks to Anwar Sadat, Menachem Begin, and Jimmy Carter in the 1970s, and Yitzhak Rabin and King Hussein in the 1990s, we have arrived. In the twenty-five years since the Egyptian-Israeli peace accord, we have moved back and forth between cold peace and cold war, but as long as the two sides are talking they don't shoot.

Imagine a group photograph of these four neighbors. Let us refer to them as the big guy, the bad guy, the little girl, and the confused good guy. The big guy in the corner is Egypt. It is the strongest and most populous Arab country, and the one that led the way to peace with Israel. Egypt's territory can contain Israel fifty times. Its population is ten times that of Israel. Its absolute GDP is smaller than that of Israel. Every four years, more new Egyptians are born than the entire population of Israel. Egypt has a "small Coptic Christian minority" numbering more than all the Jews in Israel. Let us understand this very clearly: Of the twenty-two Arab states, one has a small minority that exceeds that of the total number of Jews in Israel. So much for the Arab underdog.

The next character in the picture is the bad guy of the neighbor-hood—Syria. On a scale of zero to ten, Syria gets a clean ten as a ter-rorist state. It hosts the headquarters of Hamas and several smaller Palestinian terror organizations; it is the transfer point of all supplies to Hizbullah; it is a central player in the Iranian global terror; and, at the time of this writing, it still exerts complete colonial control over Lebanon. According to the United States, Syria is also exporting some of the merchants of death to Iraq, an activity not necessarily unrelated to the above enterprises. In a remarkable demonstration of practical wisdom, Syria has been the source of endless horrifying acts of terror, while, at the same time, firing not one shot in anger across the Syrian-Israeli border since 1975. At the same time, the Syrian economy is in a shambles. The proverbial taxi driver in me is convinced that peace be-tween Israel and Syria is just a matter of time.

When? The clocks in the Middle East run slow.

Tiny Lebanon, the little girl of the group, can barely be seen in our group photo. The ultimate playground of world hypocrisy, Lebanon was created by the French colonialists after World War I as a safe haven for Arab Christians. You might think the Christian world would have lifted a finger when Lebanon was conquered by Syria. But until very recently not one word has been uttered, and Syria continued to con-trol Lebanon. Syria has never sent an ambassador to Lebanon; it sim-ply asserts that Lebanon belongs to it. When Lebanon absorbed Palestinian refugees after the 1948 war, the Christian Palestinians were accepted as Lebanese citizens, but not the Muslims. The thankful Palestinians, led by the inevitable Arafat, triggered a long bloody reli-gious civil war, creating a state within a state in Lebanon, until Israel dismantled it in the 1980s.

The Israeli excursion into South Lebanon, which lasted almost twenty years in one form or another, was not a great success, although it did stop the repeated shelling of northern Israel. Enter the Hizbul-lah, a small, efficient, well-organized Shiite terrorist organization, armed, funded and supplied by Iran, with a strong Syrian blessing. And so little Lebanon pretends not to be conquered at all, but also pretends to be too weak to harness its resident terrorists, who control entire regions under the Syrian imprimatur. Until the fall of 2004, there has never been a single UN discussion, let alone resolution, about the unprovoked conquest of Lebanon, one of its member states, by another member state, Syria. Yet the latter occupies a seat in the Security Council, from which it pontificates about preserving world peace. It is worth noting that those who marched in the streets of Europe and the United States against America's conquest of Iraq never marched against Syria's conquest of Lebanon.

Finally, standing shy in the corner of the group picture is the unpredictable Jordan, which maintained continuous secret contact with Israel while attacking it in 1967 and supporting Saddam Hussein in the first Gulf War; which has a Palestinian majority but threw out Arafat and his gang when they tried to destroy the country in 1970; which played the pet of the Western world while ruling the West Bank from 1948 to 1967, with only Pakistan and Britain recognizing its conquest.

Egypt and Jordan are clearly on the correct side in the war against terror, while Syria and its Lebanese colony are on the wrong side. All of them are threatened, to one degree or another, by Islamic fundamentalism. Their combined population growth outperforms their economic growth—not a good formula for success. All four neighbors have an impressive cultural heritage, mostly from the pre-Islamic period but also from the glorious days when Muslim scholars were world leaders and Europe was in the Middle Ages. We should all hope and pray that one day soon they will again flourish, while continuing to control their extremist Islamic elements.

The Palestinians are absent in the group picture. They were never really allowed at the table by these four neighbors. Jordan and Egypt ruled the West Bank and Gaza for nineteen years, from 1948 until 1967, with no one uttering a word about Palestinian independence. Somehow, this was not violating anybody's rules. The Palestinians tried to destroy both Jordan and Lebanon, but in both cases they were stopped and expelled with Israel's help. The four neighbors in our picture have really never lifted a finger to help them, either in a humanitarian way or in any other way, except for offering loud condemnations on their behalf, and helping them perpetuate the refugee status of generation after generation.

One good thing that can be said about Israel's four immediate neighbors is that they are indeed neighbors. The two sides see each other, touch each other, know each other; although they have conflicting interests, they also share common borders and disputes. Whether one likes it or not, the animosity among them can be understood.

The same cannot be said for the next Arab circle, which includes Libya, Sudan, Saudi Arabia, Yemen, the Gulf States, and Iraq. They live in the same general neighborhood, but they are not Israel's next-door neighbors. A special Nobel Peace Prize should be offered to the person who can explain the puzzle of these countries. All of them are relatively far from Israel, have no border disputes with it, and should find no reason to get into a prolonged ugly conflict with it. Yet, for some reason, they are eager to inject themselves into the melee. Is this a matter of Arab solidarity? There are much bigger and more painful internal Arab disputes in the vicinity of every one of these countries, if not inside them. There are huge social problem and economic gaps within every one of them. Yet they all seem to be obsessed with the Jewish state. It is always nice to unite against the one who is different, while you and your friends are busy killing each other. It diverts attention away from your own failings.

Let us collect these characters, too, into a group snapshot. On the left we have the born-again good guy, Mr. Qaddafi, who allegedly abandoned his plans to acquire nuclear, chemical, and biological weapons. Did he really? And, excuse me for asking, but against whom was he planning to use them? Did anyone ever attack him? Perhaps the big guy, Egypt? Perhaps he wanted to liberate Sicily or Malta? Attack the United States? Russia? Perhaps he was planning to sell the weapons to his right-wing Austrian friend, Mr. Haider? This proverbial taxi driver is not sure that the last word has been said about Mr. Qaddafi's grandiose ambitions. Time will tell.

Next to this latter-day good guy we find Sudan—a nation much larger than Germany, France, Spain, Italy, and Great Britain combined. Its Arab Muslim government devotes its talents to annihilating its black Christian minority in the South and has lately turned its efforts to massacring its Muslim citizens in the West. The casualty figures there, in just the last couple of years, far exceed those of all the Israeli-Arab wars combined, over more than one hundred years. But somehow this does not really matter to the world. *Genocide, shmeno-cide*, says the United Nations; we are convening an emergency session of the General Assembly to discuss the Israeli barrier, not the Sudanese disaster. It is certain that all sides in Sudan have no interest whatsoever in Israel and its immediate neighbors, yet that fact has not prevented the Sudanese foreign minister and the Egyptian secretary general of the Arab League, Mr. Moussa (same name as the biblical Moses), to blame Israel for the trouble. Why not? When things go wrong in the Arab world, it helps to blame Israel.

And the Saudis? Can anyone explain why, when Israel's arch enemy Egypt made peace with it, the Saudis, who never had any border dispute with Israel, did not follow? Can anyone explain why the sponsor of the peace—the United States, on whom the Saudi regime entirely depends—did not pressure the Saudis to do so? Instead, the Saudis are funding the entire world terror infrastructure, from the madrassas of Indonesia to the mosques of London, even though they cannot overlook the fact that one day much of the terror they spread will end up in their own backyard.

Iraq is an unfolding story, about which much has been written and we have little to add—except to ask again: Can anyone explain why, when Saddam's 1991 invasion of Kuwait was countered by an American-led coalition that did not include Israel, Saddam's reaction was to send missiles into Israeli cities? Did he think this would improve his battlefield situation? His hold on Kuwait? Not at all.

When in trouble, says the regional wisdom, *kill the Jews.*

The situation may have been summarized best by a Catholic Paraguayan woman who was cleaning our house in Israel. Married to a South African Jew of Polish descent, she finally immigrated with him to Australia. As this living example of globalization mused to us, "Israel is a nice place, but the neighborhood?"

─11─

THE NON-ARAB CRESCENT

A moderate Iraq means an encirclement of Iran and Syria, the leading terrorist states. An abandoned Iraq would create a huge Iranian Empire.

The Koran is written in Arabic. Most Muslims are not Arabs, do not speak Arabic, and cannot read the Koran. Many of them are now being fed whatever certain fanatical preachers want them to hear. This regrettable situation has been repeatedly addressed by moderate Arab leaders such as King Abdullah of Jordan.

From Turkey to Nigeria and from Bangladesh to Indonesia, the Sunni preachers (largely financed by Saudi money) and the Shiites (mostly energized by Iran) are transmitting more and more extreme messages. They urge a variety of actions against the infidels, which include the "Crusaders" (i.e., Christians) and the Jews (i.e., Jews). The messages are addressed not only to Arab devotees, but also to the majority of Muslims, Arab or otherwise, who enjoyed until recently a very mild and nonbelligerent Islam. Vicious anti-American incitement has now been added to the menu. Anyone who has read excerpts of these fiery speeches might find it difficult to believe that this is the twenty-first century. But it is.

It would be absolutely outrageous for me to express opinions about the Koran or any other religious issue connected with Islam. I do not even qualify to make such judgments about Judaism, a culture in which I have lived all my life. I should certainly refrain from addressing Islamic issues.

But one thing is clear: The flames of violent incitement are spreading within the Muslim world, which is far greater, wider, and stronger than the Arab world. In fact, the three largest Muslim nations in the world—Indonesia, Bangladesh, and Pakistan—are not Arab. Each of them, as well as India's Muslim minority, has more Muslim citizens than Egypt, the largest Arab nation. But there are two other important Muslim countries, which are not Arab and which are approximately equal in population to Egypt. These countries are the key to our discussion here: Iran and Turkey.

Iran and Turkey are the two ends of the outer crescent, which embraces the Middle East. Both of them are very large countries. Turkey covers an area roughly the size of Italy and Spain combined. Iran is larger than France, Germany, Italy, and the United Kingdom combined. Each one of them has a population ten times that of Israel. In each one, the largest city (Tehran and Istanbul) is more populous than all of Israel. Turkey has the second largest military force among the NATO countries after the United States, and ahead of any Western European country. Iran is militarily strong, possesses homemade long-range missiles, and is trying to develop nuclear weapons, using its own technology as well as imported ones from North Korea and Pakistan.

No two Muslim countries are more different from each other than these two non-Arab giants. Until recently, Turkey has been the living example that a Muslim country can be democratic and reasonably successful. Thanks to the father of modern Turkey, Ataturk, it has a secular constitution. It takes pride in being partly in Europe, and is eager to join the European Union. It maintains good relations with Israel, and has been in the Western camp throughout the entire Cold War. It has suffered from terror and has never been involved in defending or even in tolerating the Islamic terror infrastructure in any way, direct or indirect.

The problem is that Turkey has lately been moving in the wrong direction, with an Islamic party winning its recent election and a successful invasion of Islamic fanaticism beginning to make inroads into the general public. In Germany and other European countries, it is sad—actually pathetic—to see Turkish immigrants, who always wanted to merge into the local culture, now suddenly adopting head scarves and other religious symbols, which did not characterize them until recently.

Who is funding this campaign? The same sources that fund similar campaigns in Muslim communities all around the world.

There is another serious problem in Turkey. The Turkish constitution is totally secular. But, in times of stress, the real guardian of the constitution has often been the Turkish military. This does not sound very democratic, and Europeans consider it an absolute abomination. Yet if not for the Turkish army, the fact is that Turkey might have already become a "standard" undemocratic Muslim country, at the doorstep of Europe. This is yet another case in which applying the normal rules of the great democracies may lead to a disaster in a fragile society. Turkey is eager to join the European Union. The European Union insists that civil liberties, human rights, and true democracy are absolute conditions for admission, which sounds very reasonable.

But if Turkey were to follow these rules to the letter, it might allow the Islamic parties to gain complete control of the country, reversing the Ataturk revolution, changing the constitution, and converting Turkey into yet another fanatic Islamic state, which certainly would not qualify to join the EU. This would be a classic case of a democracy destroying itself. However, European support for Turkey's current constitution, and anyone who is fighting to preserve it, may sound like interfering in the internal affairs of another country, and might contradict fundamental theories about democracy. But it might also save almost seventy million Turks from moving their entire country into an earlier century. It's a difficult choice, but Europe can make or break Turkey.

Iran and its present regime is the number one danger to the world today. It has definite ambitions to rule a vast area, and to expand in all directions. It has an ideology that claims supremacy over Western culture. It is ruthless, and has proven that it can use its embassies to execute elaborate terrorist acts without leaving too many traces. Its so-called moderates and conservatives play their own virtuoso version of the good cop-bad cop game. Iran sponsors Syrian terrorism; it is behind much of the action in Iraq; it fully funds the Hizbullah and, through it, the Palestinian Hamas and Islamic Jihad; it has perpetrated acts of terror in Europe and South America, and probably also in Uzbekistan and Saudi Arabia. It leads a multinational terror consortium that includes, as minor players, Syria, Lebanon, and certain Shiite elements in Iraq. In addition, I am not at all sure we know all the facts concerning indirect Iranian involvement in al Qaida and the September 11 attacks. Yes, Iran is Shiite and al Qaida is Sunni. But it is a fact that the Sunni Hamas and Islamic Jihad are both directly supported by the Shiite Hizbullah.

Decades ago, before the Khomeini revolution, Iran was run ruthlessly by the Shah and his friends. They were supported by the entire Western world, led by the United States and including Israel, who always tried to establish the best possible relations with non-Arab Muslim countries. If I suspected the Iranian leaders of being very emotional and impractical, I would have believed that this is the reason for their relentless campaign against the United States and Israel, which they call "The Great Satan" and "The Little Satan." But I have much more respect for the sophistication and pragmatism of the Iranian leaders. They are clearly interested in Israel only as a vehicle of securing their influence in the Arab world and possibly achieving an overall hegemony in the Middle East. There is no better scapegoat than Israel, if this is your goal. They view Europe as "a continent for sale," where generous business contracts can secure continued inaction on the European side. They are delighted to see America diving into the Iraqi mess, where Iran can incite the Shiite majority and support Sunni terror with little effort, getting the United States into real trouble.

Nevertheless, most European countries still trade with Iran, trying to appease it while refusing to read the clear signals—even as Iran continues to show great talent in manipulating the gullible European governments.

If we look at the map of the Middle East, two extreme scenarios present themselves. The optimistic scenario is that Turkey remains a secular democracy, with a strong antiterror posture, and Iraq ends up as a moderate Muslim country, with some degree of democracy and a pro-Western inclination. In this case, Iran is surrounded by forces that are hostile to it and its plans: In the east a "born-again" Afghanistan, in the north the Muslim former Soviet republics, in the west Iraq, and in the south the Gulf states. Syria is likewise surrounded by Turkey in the north, Iraq in the east, Jordan and Israel in the south, and the sea in the west. Lebanon, for the time being, is part of Syria.

I have no idea whether the U.S. attack on Iraq was partly motivated by these strategic geographical considerations. They have certainly not been mentioned in public. It is entirely possible that this theory is a matter of 20/20 hindsight. But if one looks at the Iraq invasion as a part of a World War III, then its most important result is the encircling of Iran and Syria, a necessary step for any containment of these safe havens of terror.

This brings us to the horrifying, but not unrealistic, pessimistic scenario. If the United States and its allies leave Iraq and an Iranian-inspired Shiite regime is established there, and if Turkey continues to drift toward fanatic Islam and away from its traditional policies, the result would be a huge, continuous area dominated by Iran. This area would include not only Iran but Iraq, Syria, and Lebanon. It would have a population of 110 million, all the oil reserves of Iran, Iraq, and Syria, access to both the Indian Ocean and the Mediterranean, and missiles that can reach anywhere in Europe. And that is leaving aside the prospect of nuclear weapons, and the most elaborate terror network ever created. This would surely lead to a full-fledged, all encompassing world war, whether World War III or World War IV I cannot tell.

If Turkey should remain neutral in such a scenario—let alone supporting the Iranian conglomerate—Europe, with its large and growing Muslim minorities, would be in real danger.

Of course, real life usually doesn't follow either the most optimistic or the most pessimistic scenario. Endless additional factors intervene, and the ability of leaders to make mistakes should not be underestimated. Among the many factors we have not considered are the internal developments in Iran itself. There is clearly a growing unrest, among various influential elements in the Iranian society, against the corrupt and fanatic regime of the Ayatollahs. This does not mean that Iran will become a democracy tomorrow, but it is an important variable in the equation. Another important element is the Kurds, who are a very large, troublesome minority from the point of view of Turkey, Iraq, Iran, and Syria. The Kurds themselves believe that they are entitled to their own independent state. (*Why should they?* The argument goes. *They are not Palestinians.* That they outnumber the Palestinians is, of course, immaterial.) There is also another important neighbor in the region: Russia. Although demoted from superpower status, Russia is still a power, and would be very nervous to see an emerging nuclear Islamic Empire forming on its southern border. Finally, the mad rush of Iran toward nuclear weapons may give a wake-up call to some Western powers, before it is too late. All of these issues are imponderable and hard to sort out. The uncertainty is enormous, and so are the stakes.

The Jewish tradition says that, since the destruction of the Jewish temple in Jerusalem, prophecies were only empowered to fools. Thus it's a good idea to steer clear of making predictions—except to underline the crucial importance of bringing the very problematic Iraqi adventure to a successful close.

~12~

FREEDOM FRIES

When America wakes up, Europe is out to lunch.

At the age of twenty-four, after receiving my PhD in theoretical physics in Israel, I went to the United States for the first time. On my first evening there, I had dinner with friends in an obscure restaurant in the small town of Westmont, Illinois. I was quite fluent in English, but my teachers did not prepare me for what would happen next. When I ordered a salad, the kind waitress looked me straight in the eye and asked: "French, Roquefort, Thousand Islands?" An uncertain question mark dangled at the end of this amazing sentence. I knew that Roquefort was a French cheese, but I didn't think it came from the islands, and I couldn't figure out where one might encounter a thousand such islands. When my reaction suggested that she was facing an imbecile, the waitress became impatient, and angrily mumbled something about "dressing." I was properly dressed, I didn't want any cheese, there was nothing French in Westmont, Illinois, and I knew for a fact that we were in the middle of the continental United States, far from any islands.

As I became more enlightened, I realized that French dressing, French fries, and French toast are staples of American cuisine—even though their American names, if not their taste, would induce indigestion in any self-respecting Frenchman. I can imagine the relief of the French, in the winter of 2003, when all such items were temporarily renamed "Freedom Toast" and the like, freeing the French from any association with them. At the same time, the vintners of Napa Valley gloried at the sight of good French wine being poured down the drain.

While all of this was happening, the French minister of foreign affairs, Dominique de Villepin, adamantly refused to answer journalists who asked whether he sided with George W. Bush or Saddam Hussein in the ongoing dispute that led to the Iraq War. If I may add the personal view of this proverbial taxi driver: Renaming *pommes frites* is silly, and destroying good wine is an act against humanity—but both pale in comparison with the outrageously "even-handed" attitude of Mr. Villepin.

When the text of my speech started circulating on the Internet, one of the first sites that posted it was something called (please excuse me; I didn't make this up) "fuckfrance.com." For every such anti-European sentiment I heard, however, the amazing hostility of so many Europeans to the United States was even more disturbing. Something has gone very wrong between the two main pillars of the free world. Blaming Bush and/or Chirac for it is a gross oversimplification. This was clearly an outburst waiting to happen; Iraq was merely a good excuse.

I never thought that one party in a dispute could be at once more sophisticated and more naïve than its rival. But this was the role played by Europe during the lead-up to the Iraq War. In one way or another, the United States has been at war almost continuously since World War II—from the Cold War to Korea, Vietnam, the first Gulf War, to the military involvements in Berlin, Lebanon, Grenada, Somalia, and Kosovo. More important, throughout those years American soldiers have been permanently stationed in Germany, Japan, Britain, Korea, the Gulf States, and elsewhere (although never in Israel). America had its finger on the nuclear trigger for decades, as long as the Soviet Empire existed.

For better or worse, then, America knows what a war is. It has learned many important lessons, even if not all of them were internalized. As any Israeli knows, war is ugly, terrible, painful, and dangerous, but it is preferable to annihilation. The Americans have spent decades learning this lesson, although their idea of annihilation has never been as literal as that of the Israelis, who are all too familiar with the idea of genuine extinction.

In the meantime, the Europeans, licking their severe wounds after World War II, were conveniently protected against the Soviet Empire by the Americans. The lesson they learned, rightly or wrongly, was that one could flourish without fighting, and without even maintaining a real army. At the height of the Cold War, one small political party in Denmark ran an election campaign whose platform seriously recommended replacing the Danish defense budget with a single recorded message to be played on all radio stations in case of an attack: "We surrender." Clearly, the leaders of this party have not spent much time in a Gulag.

The older Europeans remember World War II and its horrors. The young ones have not the faintest idea what war is. It is amazing, but the Syrian army, certainly not the strongest in the Middle East, supported by the collapsing economy of a poor country, may be stronger than the armies of Germany or France.

They might not have wanted to remember it, but the French and the Germans knew that the only reason they were living in peace and freedom, prospering despite the fact that they had no serious army, is the fact that the United States had protected them for decades against the Soviet Union. This was even truer for the Belgians, Danes, and Austrians. Any beginning student of human psychology would tell you that too profound a reliance on another usually leads to big trouble. As long as the Soviet Empire was on the horizon, Europeans might have harbored resentment over this dependency on America, but they rarely voiced it. Once the Evil Empire was gone, however, all inhibitions were removed, and the explosion was simply waiting for a match to ignite it.

One clear sign that Europe completely failed to understand the Cold War had to do with Israel. While the Europeans were actively protected by American troops on European soil, paid by American tax-payers, Israel has never been protected by American troops. The financial military support it received from the United States was far smaller than America's investment in the defense of wealthy Western Europe. Yet that never stopped many Europeans from repeatedly and contemptuously proclaiming that Israel was defended by the United States and would collapse without it. These critics truly didn't want to accept that their own defense was handsomely paid for by the Americans, and that their good life was guaranteed by thousands of American missiles and bombs and by hundreds of thousands of American soldiers stationed in Europe. In this world, there are not only proverbial scientists and taxi drivers, but also proverbial camels—and, as the Arab proverb says, "The camel does not see his own hump."

So, in many ways, Europe grew to be truly naïve when it came to matters of life and death, war and peace. The children of upper-middle-class Mom and Dad are often unaware that their parents had to struggle hard in order to give them such a good life. They take such things for granted. Europe believed that commercial relations were more important than any long-range principles, and that every conflict could be settled through pleasant conversation over a glass of Bordeaux or Schnapps. The Americans know better. The Soviets and the Islamic terrorists also know otherwise. Even the Eastern European countries, which recently joined the European Union, know that you must fight to win freedom and depose a corrupt and oppressive regime. Western Europe has yet to understand this, in practice, if not in theory.

At the same time, Europeans have always considered themselves much more sophisticated than their American allies. In a way, they are. Shakespeare, Voltaire, and Goethe, they think, have no American equivalents. The Americans are not mature enough to understand that the sex adventures of politicians are minor human footnotes to life, that showing women's breasts on TV is nothing to write home about, that four-letter words should not be deleted in print and beeped on broadcast, and that catching a politician in a reasonable lie and minor corruption is no big surprise. The Europeans also want it noted that they exported espresso, Verdi, and Modigliani to America, and got McDonald's, Elvis, and Snoopy in return.

As an Israeli scientist, I have been invited to participate in many European Union science policy meetings, discussing the large knowledge gap between the United States and the EU. The high-tech arena is almost entirely dominated by the Americans, and very few European research organizations can compete favorably with their American parallels. In fact, during the entire period of the high-tech "bubble" of the late 1990s, little Israel had more start-up companies than the entire EU. European universities are almost always owned by government, assuring a certain uniformity and, alas, mediocrity, while American universities and colleges range from the best in the world to the worst. In a world whose economy is almost entirely knowledge-based, these are very serious matters. While Europe talks nonstop about competitiveness, innovation, and other buzzwords, they've done little to bridge the Atlantic gap.

As a citizen of Israel and of Globania, whether speaking as a scientist or a taxi driver, I do not want to choose between America and Europe, any more than one wants to choose between Mom and Dad. I love them both, and I don't want to see them divorce. If there is a future to Globania, it relies on the unity and harmony, with reasonable competition, of the two giants.

In considering the European attitude toward the emerging world war, another important element should not be overlooked. Europe has a huge Muslim minority, partly Arab and partly non-Arab (the latter being mainly Turks in Germany and Pakistanis in Britain). This minority is growing at a rapid pace, both by immigration, legal and illegal, and by a much higher birth rate, in contrast with the negative population growth of many of their host countries. The pace is such that Belgium may become the second Muslim republic in Europe, after Albania. This leads to "Islamophobia," to uncertainty, but also to an increasing attention to a growing Muslim vote in the elections.

It is absolutely reasonable and expected that a devout Muslim might wish to remain devout after immigrating to Europe. It is also understandable that other immigrants, whatever their religion, might want to assimilate and reduce their loyalty to their religion. But the disturbing trend in Europe is that the fundamentalism of many Muslim immigrants is increasing, not diminishing or remaining steady. This is not good news at all, and when Europe returns from lunch it may be rather late.

France and Italy are separated from North Africa by the Mediterranean. Had a miracle, or an environmental catastrophe, dried this sea, both countries would have undoubtedly built a barrier between the French Riviera and Sicily on one side and North Africa on the other. Such a barrier would make the now-famous Israeli barrier look like a small hedge. In fact, with the sea still in place, the issue of blocking desperate North Africans from arriving into the European Union by boats is already on the agenda. The admission of Turkey into the EU hinges on related issues, even if most European leaders are trying to deny it. The immigration policies of many European countries are being revised. Again, the new Eastern European members of the EU are free from these considerations, having been unattractive to immigration until now.

As long as life is good, as long as the only suicide murders are in Israel, Iraq, the United States, and other distant locations, Europe may continue to pretend that there is no war. The March 2004 bombings in Madrid killed two hundred people and convinced the Spanish public to surrender to terror. Books claiming that September 11 was a CIA plot were circulated widely in France. This will not be remembered as Europe's finest hour.

Demonizing Israel is another convenient way to deny reality. It is a wonderful mixture of covert anti-Semitism, self-compensation for "Islamophobia," a side-blow to America, supporting the underdog (Don't they own an atlas in Europe?), and the aforementioned, infamous even-handedness of people like de Villepin. "Since Hamas, Hizbullah and al Qaida are real bad guys, Israel must be the same," says the enlightened even-handed European.

But even Europe will wake up. The 2004 murder of the Dutch filmmaker Theo Van Gogh by a Muslim terrorist, who did not like what he had seen in the movies, alerted Europe to some of the dangers. The French deportation of an inciting Muslim preacher was another minor turning point. The sophisticated and self-controlled French, who always reprimand Israeli reactions to the murder of civilians and to the blowing up of supermarkets and buses, have now demonstrated their own legendary restraint by destroying the entire air force of the Ivory Coast after several of their soldiers were accidentally killed.

The fact that the United States is the world's one and only super-power—and the arrogance this role invites—is no help in the transat-lantic melee. If your next-door neighbor is strong, arrogant, and *nouveau riche*, it's going to be difficult to like him that much and easy to look for excuses to yell at him. But if your well-being depends on the harmony between you and him, better forget all of these petty attitudes.

America has its own denial groups. There are those who mix their own polarized internal politics with the illusion that Iran does not exist, Hamas is a welfare organization, and the world would be nicer if Asia and Africa could be forgotten. Well, that isn't going to happen. Ameri-cans should learn that you can allow abortions, believe in the Big Bang, and oppose tax breaks for high-income earners, while still realizing that the three-ring circus of Islamic terror is a serious threat to America, to the world, and to the well-being, at home, of the individual citizen.

There is only one way to win against the terror networks and erase them from the face of the earth: An absolute, united commitment among the nations of the free world to eliminating the ringleaders, iso-lating and even liberating the countries who support terrorists, and, most important, finding educational and social ways of emancipating women, banning the indoctrination of children, preventing systematic brainwashing by media, and opening the relevant countries to the world at large.

In that long sentence, the most important phrase is "an absolute, united commitment among the nations of the free world." I believe this will happen, either through the strong efforts and shared vision of leaders on both sides of the Atlantic, or as a result of terrorist attacks in Europe that could dwarf September 11. I prefer, by far, the first option.

—13—

DOES THE SUN RISE
IN THE EAST?

*The incredible economy of China creates an entirely new
"South Korea" every three years. Why can't the rest of the poor
rural areas of the world do the same?*

When I landed in Beijing Airport for the first time, I handed my Israeli passport to the Chinese Immigration Officer. He gave it a quick look, smiled, and said: "Israel! Einstein!" What on earth did he mean? I wondered. Obviously, he could not have known that I happened to be a theoretical physicist, a guest of the Chinese Academy of Science. Although he was Jewish, Einstein was not an Israeli.

When I asked my Chinese colleagues and hosts about this strange incident, however, they knew the answer immediately. When you visit a museum in China, it turns out there are three different admission prices: one for Chinese, one for foreigners, and one for "overseas Chinese"—or, in Jewish terminology, the Diaspora. Overseas Chinese can be Canadian, Vietnamese, or Swedish. They may have been born in China, in their country of citizenship, or elsewhere. They may live in a poor Chinatown, or be wealthy tycoons.

But in all cases they are "overseas Chinese," and China feels a special kinship to them.

So that was the answer: From the Chinese point of view, Einstein was the most famous and admired "overseas Israeli." The Chinese immigration officer intuitively understood what most of the world refused to digest: Israel is the home of the Jews, even though many of them live abroad, some of them don't like Israel, and some of them will never visit it. Just like China, only a few hundred times smaller.

A year later, I was invited to lecture in a multidisciplinary conference in Tokyo. I had dinner with a Japanese government minister and a few other international scholars of different fields and nationalities. The Japanese host was surprised to discover that most of the people around the dinner table, all selected by the Japanese conference organizers, happened to be Jewish. In the ensuing conversation, I told our host an old story about the five Jews who changed the world. The first was Moses, who based his teachings on the brain. Next was Jesus, whose teachings were centered on the heart. The third prominent Jew, Karl Marx, based everything on the stomach. The fourth Jew, Sigmund Freud, went further down in the human body. Finally, the fifth Jew, Albert Einstein, pointed out that everything was relative. The Japanese minister looked puzzled and did not produce even a faint smile. "He never realized that these people were Jewish," I thought to myself. I asked him politely and carefully if there was anything strange about the story. "Yes," he said "but Moses was Egyptian."

China and Japan are world powers. They are far from the Middle East and they have almost no Jewish communities. They see nearly everything differently from the Western world. Unlike Christians and Muslims, they do not get very emotional about matters related to the Jews. If Jesus was Jewish, Moses was indeed Egyptian. If Moses was Jewish, Jesus was Christian. If Einstein is Jewish and Israel is the land of the Jews, then Einstein is an overseas Israeli. The logic is perfect. The Chinese and the Japanese aren't particularly interested in who should be blamed for the crucifixion two thousand years ago. They don't understand why Palestinian refugees are more important than tens of millions of refugees in East Asia. The Holocaust is for them a sad chapter in the history of others, unrelated to them. And when you find in Japanese bookstores copies of *The Protocols of the Elders of Zion*, the most famous anti-Semitic forgery and lie of all times, it reflects the very peculiar anti-Semitism of people who have almost never seen a Jew. In fact, says the Japanese logic, if the Jews indeed control the entire world, perhaps one should admire them, not hate them. All of this sounds very bizarre to American, European, or Middle Eastern ears. It is all very far from the storm.

But Japan, South Korea, and China do offer an extremely interesting model of how to solve the economic gap problems of Globania. One hundred years ago, these countries were desperately poor, far behind the Western powers. Today, all three are in different stages of participating in the knowledge revolution.

Japan has become the second-largest economy in the world, with its own very special brand of outstanding technology and good education. The 130 million Japanese are clearly among the 1 billion citizens of Globania, who are full participants in the knowledge revolution and who have acquired wealth and good living conditions as a result. Japan has reached this goal in spite of having no natural resources, and in spite of being extremely crowded. At the risk of oversimplifying a complex subject and generalizing national characteristics, it might be said that the secret formula of Japan includes discipline, loyalty, precision, learning from others, hard teamwork, competitiveness, and the willingness and ability to reorient a culture in order to achieve goals.

South Korea has its own brand of technological and economic progress, placing it behind Japan, but on the threshold of joining the affluent nations. Its per capita GDP is higher than that of Saudi Arabia and approaching that of Greece and Portugal. The 50 million South Koreans are producing about one-quarter of what 1.2 billion Chinese do. Korea, in a phrase, is turning into the Poland of the East. Poland is sandwiched between the two giants, Russia and Germany. Despite being almost continually dominated by one or the other for centuries, Poland has managed to preserve its culture; now, at last, it is on a path of gradual progress and development. The same can be said for Korea, which had been repeatedly occupied and dominated by the Japanese or the Chinese since time immemorial.

China is the fastest-growing economy on earth and is already the second largest energy-consuming nation. The Chinese have the longest surviving continuous history and culture of any nation, longer than the Jews or anyone else. But China still has almost one billion rural inhabitants, who are extremely poor and largely unaware of global developments. It is a great achievement that these people already produce enough food and very basic needs for themselves, but their overall contribution to the Chinese economy is very small, and they are clearly among the four billion nonparticipants in the technology revolution that created Globania.

As a guest of the Chinese Academy, I learned that, while China's population is two hundred times that of Israel and its GDP is fifteen times that of Israel, its annual research and development expenditure is only three times that of Israel. However, every year 20 million Chinese children attend school for the first time. The Chinese first-graders alone outnumber all Israeli citizens three to one.

We keep hearing, year after year, that the Chinese GDP is growing at an amazing annual rate of 8 to 10 percent. Even a proverbial taxi driver understands that in order to produce 10 percent more, you must either have 10 percent more people producing at the same level, have every person producing 10 percent more, or somehow combine the two. But the population of China grows very slowly, thanks to the totalitarian regime's strict population-control measures. Can we believe that every average Chinese worker in Beijing improves his or her productivity, year after year, by 10 percent? This is totally unreasonable. So if the population does not increase and the productivity of the individual industrial or agricultural worker cannot increase so significantly, for so many years, what is happening here?

The solution of the puzzle is a lesson to be transmitted to the rest of the poor nations of the world. China consists of a little more than 200 million people with the average productivity of, say, South Korea, and a billion citizens who produce almost nothing but have enough to eat. At the risk of gross oversimplification, you might say the Chinese economy has 200 million "participants" and about one billion "nonparticipants." The participants are as wealthy and as educated as the Koreans; the nonparticipants are totally remote from the global knowledge revolution.

The growth of the Chinese economy is based not on an increase of the overall population, but on an increase in the number of people joining the ranks of those who contribute. The others may not be hungry or unemployed, exactly, but their contribution to the economy is negligible. Schematically speaking, if every year an additional 20 million people join the ranks of the participants, the economy grows by 10 percent, even if every "participant worker" remains as productive or unproductive as he or she was a year earlier.

In terms of economic data, roughly speaking, China comprises four South Koreas and a billion peasants. But every three years an entire new additional economic South Korea is created within China. This happens by a complex process of urbanization and education, accompanied by added infrastructure, environmental problems, and the emergence of all the ills of big cities. It is not clear how long this can proceed at the present pace, but so far there is no slowdown. In many ways, China and Japan are as different as any two nations can be, but in economic terms China is also as impressive as Japan. Chinese progress, like Japanese progress, is based on hard work, education, and talent. But it is also based on individualism, a relatively undisciplined but very energetic chaotic behavior, a lot of entrepreneurial spirit, and an immense talent in the special national sport of beating the system.

There is clearly more than one path to success, and it is crucial to the future of Globania that its different ethnic groups preserve their special characteristics. It is clear that the chaotic, entrepreneurial Jews are much more like the Chinese, while the disciplined and precise Germans may be superficially more similar to the Japanese. All of these cultures are extremely successful, each in its own way.

But all cultures that succeed have certain common attributes: They learn from other cultures and technologies; they do not blame others for their own failures; they invest in education and learning; they recognize that progress can be achieved only through very hard work, not through incitement and lies. In one sentence: As long as you do not suffer from intellectual poverty, you can overcome economic poverty.

All of which makes it so sad to see how, in the Arab world, millions of rural people are also moving into the big cities—but, instead of becoming "educated contributors," their first act is to supplement their poor shack with a satellite dish, giving them continuous access to a nonstop barrage of hatred, lies, and ignorance.

Such observations, of course, are necessarily general and superficial. They paint the picture with a very wide brush, offering only a glimpse of the relevance of the Far East to our storm. The number one task of all Globanians is to reveal the positive lessons that can be found in the stories of Japan, China, and Korea, and to suggest their relevance to the billions of nonparticipants. Their success is ours. Their fate is ours. If gigantic China can move forward at this pace, perhaps the rest of the world can learn something.

But China and Japan are not the only players in East Asia. There are also almost 300 million Muslims, primarily in Indonesia and Malaysia but also in other countries, including China itself. The East Asian Muslim communities were, until recently, on a positive track. But now the fanatical preachers in the mosques and madrassas have reached them. The traditionally mild forms of Islam are being slowly replaced by fiery rhetoric and by a determined attempt to push what could have been successful nations back into intellectual poverty. They are only just beginning their efforts, again funded primarily by Saudi money, but if they are not stopped, major disasters might follow. The determination of the Muslim governments of countries like Indonesia and Malaysia to fight against terror is crucial, but it is not at all clear that the leaders in the region understand its importance.

In the midst of all this, one important island—both literally and economically—is Singapore, where a small nation of primarily "overseas Chinese" has established itself with great success in the midst of the huge Muslim surroundings. Let us hope that the spread of militant Islam will not create yet another eye of the storm in that part of the world.

—14—

RIGHT IS WRONG

The Book of Psalms says: "If I forget thee Jerusalem, let my right be forgotten." My advice: Don't forget Jerusalem, but forget the right.

There is only one political struggle in which I would like everybody to be an extremist: The fight against extremism. It is the extremists who always fight for their ideas. The vast majority in the broad political center, whether moderate right or moderate left, opposes extremism, but without the fervor of those at the political fringes. Extremists lie without blushing, while in the political center it is more difficult and less acceptable to do so. Extremists are always getting attention in the news, by making outrageous statements, by organizing loud, well-reported demonstrations, or by performing real atrocities. As a result, extremism flourishes and has a much stronger media echo than its sheer numerical weight justifies.

In mathematics, arguments can be carried to their bitter logical end, often yielding absolute black or white results and giving rise to an extreme position. This is not so in real life and in human situations. If the real world were a black-and-white movie, the dominant color would be gray. Human problems are far too complex, and depend on too many factors, to resolve easily into a set of absolute precepts. Any extreme view of human nature is an oversimplification, and sometimes it can be an act of blindness.

It is interesting that the positions of the far Left and the far Right often coincide, as if politics were played on a circle, not on a straight line. As in circling the earth, those who move far enough to the right politically will reach the extreme left, and vice versa. It is not an accident that the full name of Nazism was National Socialism, an unholy marriage of right and left terminology. The Molotov-Ribentrop pact was a telling, if short-lived, marriage of Nazi Germany and Communist Russia.

In the United States, George W. Bush is outflanked on the right by Pat Buchanan, who considers Israel a permanent source of evil and simply cannot conceal his pathological hatred of the Jewish state. Thousands of miles away, the extreme right-wing Russian political forces are viciously anti-Semitic and anti-Israeli. It is amusing, or perhaps not so amusing, to read Buchanan happily quoting the attacks of the Israeli far Left on Prime Minister Sharon. One may not like Sharon, but the meeting of minds between Buchanan and the Israeli far Left, like that between the Russian Communists and the Fascists, is an unholy alliance. Finally, Ralph Nader, who has outflanked John Kerry on the left, agrees with Buchanan that Israel is the mother of all evil. Nice people.

The Jews have long been targeted by European Fascists and Nazis, by the American Ku Klux Klan, and by racists of all stripes. The Palestinian leadership, along with major Arab leaders in Iraq and Egypt, actively supported Hitler in the 1930s and 1940s. After World War II, many Nazis escaped and found refuge in Syria and Egypt. The roots of much of today's Muslim terror go back to the Muslim Brothers, an organization founded decades ago in Egypt and strongly supported by the Nazis.

The Russian Tsarists allowed and encouraged the pogroms of pre–Soviet Russia, and the most conservative wings of the Catholic

Church never missed an anti-Jewish occasion and never spoke up during the Holocaust. The Saudi oil-dripping version of fanatic Islam certainly belongs to the same league, using forged Tsarist-era defamation literature and Nazi-style cartoons to defame Israel and the Jews.

You might think that the regrettable "Islamophobia" practiced today by so many right-wing parties in Europe might lead them to have sympathies for Israel and for its struggle against fanatic Islamic terror. Not at all. Killing Jews does not constitute terrorism, according to some of these parties. It is a liberation movement, even if it means attacking a synagogue in Istanbul. These European bigots cannot free themselves from their anti-Semitic, anti-Israeli prejudices, and they will not let mere facts confuse them. Austria's Joerg Haider is a good friend of Saddam Hussein and Muammar Qaddafi; anti-Semitism is the only issue that gets him into the same bed with his far Left rivals. His counterparts in France, Switzerland, the Netherlands, and elsewhere are not any better.

There are many more white racists than black racists in the world, although both kinds exist. But they all hate the Jews and Israel. There are European racists who hate the Muslims, and Muslim racists who hate Christians and blacks. But all of them hate the Jews and Israel. It leads one to wonder whether God created the Jews to give all of these "beautiful" people something to agree about.

The Israeli right wing is not improving the situation. As we shall argue later, there is nothing sacred about Israel's 1967 borders, but to deliberately build isolated small settlements in densely populated Palestinian areas is stupid, infuriating, and untenable. That earlier Israeli governments had illusions about this issue may be understandable. But there is a big difference between an Israeli town in an empty area of the West Bank and a settlement whose only purpose is to establish a presence where none belongs, in the midst of a crowded Palestinian area. It is clear that these isolated settlements have no future, and their establishment was a bad mistake from any reasonable point of view; but it will still take a long time and a lot of Israeli infighting before they are dismantled.

The Israeli far Right is as bad as the far Right anywhere else. To even think, let alone speak, about transferring the Palestinian population from the Palestinian areas into neighboring countries is immoral, inhuman, and contradicts anything decent people believe in, no matter what the Palestinians do. It is also impractical, although that should not matter at all. To attack innocent Palestinians deliberately is very wrong, even when a war is raging, although one cannot avoid hurting people accidentally, while destroying the terrorists. To contemplate any damage to Islamic holy shrines is exactly as vicious as to do the same for sacred Jewish or Christian places. Even if one side does it, the other side should never even consider it.

The bad news is that a small minority of Israelis does think that way, according to the results of all recent elections. The good news is that the vast majority thinks otherwise. But the right-wing fanatic minority is causing major damage to the just causes of Israel, which has been fighting for its life for generations. The massacre of praying Palestinians in Hebron by an Israeli terrorist, who died on the spot, and the murder of Prime Minister Rabin by another Israeli terrorist, who will hopefully rot in jail for the rest of his life, were isolated but horrific warning signs during the 1990s. The fact that these were the only major Israeli acts of terror in many years of bitter fighting is no consolation to anyone.

There are indications today that some elements in the Israeli Right wing might go as far as imitating the Islamic terrorists, performing equally murderous acts against anyone who does not agree with them, Arab or Jewish. Those who advocate such acts in the future should be dealt with as firmly as any other terrorist.

Two wrongs do not make a right. But two rights can produce a wrong. The fact that the European, the American, the Russian, and the Arab extreme Right are so hostile to the Israeli extreme Right does not make any of them right.

⤙15⤚

LEFT BEHIND

The political far Left has always claimed to be the avant-garde. How is it that in all matters of the Middle East, it supports the most backward and archaic forces of discrimination and inequality?

We were having dinner with a group of enlightened Europeans. "Should Turkey be admitted to the European Union?" someone asked. "It must first demonstrate that it believes in, and exercises, human rights, civil liberties, and full democracy," said another. I pointed out that the latest result of democracy in Turkey was an Islamic party running the government and a marked increase in the number of women who are required to wear head scarves. "But this is what these women voted for," said a Scandinavian woman, although I know she considers equal rights for women a sacred principle and would be willing to take on anyone who challenged it.

There is no clearer demonstration of the hypocrisy or naïveté of the intellectual European Left when it comes to the Middle East. How is it possible that women's organizations in Europe observe the status of women in the Islamic world without raising a voice? If anyone dared to accuse a raped European woman of contributing to the rape by wearing a provocative outfit, he would be considered an outcast, and rightfully so, by any reasonable person. But every day in the Arab world women are murdered (yes, murdered) by their brothers (yes, their real brothers) simply because their rape "stains the honor of the family." The murderers are not punished because they have fulfilled their duty, and the rapists are rarely found.

Clearly, Muslim women have never voted for such treatment. Nor have they voted for being prevented from driving a car in Saudi Arabia, or for needing permission from their husbands if they want to leave their countries. Nor have they voted for wearing a black head-to-toe outfit with tiny holes for the eyes, or for being prohibited from attending school. And if they did cast votes for such violations of basic human rights, it was certainly not of their own free will—at best it was because they were brainwashed by their lifetime of immersion in this repressive culture.

Why are European women (and men) not demonstrating daily in front of these Muslim nations' embassies? Why aren't women's organizations demanding UN resolutions that boycott the offending countries? Are the principles of women's equality applicable to only Europeans and Americans? And, sadly, why is it far more common to see delegations of feminist organizations in anti-Israeli demonstrations, whether in San Francisco or in Berlin, and to hear condemnations of Israel in international conferences on women's issues?

For that matter, why aren't "green" environmental organizations targeting the oil countries with their criticism? Is there anyone who wastes energy and pollutes the oceans and the beaches more than some of these countries? Are they exempt from criticism because they are not European? If, according to environmental organizations, nuclear power stations are bad for Europe and America, why don't these groups protest Iran's desire to build one, even though the country swims in oil? Instead, the green parties can usually be found in the front ranks of any criticism on Israel.

Israeli universities allow for total academic freedom. Their professors may level even the most vicious criticism and accusations at anything their government is doing or has done. In the Arab world, not only is there no academic freedom and no freedom of speech, but also in the universities of Egypt—a country that made peace with Israel decades ago—scholars have been prevented for years from collaborating or communicating with their Israeli counterparts. Do we hear any complaints about this in Europe or America? Not at all. There are only calls for boycotting Israeli scholars and Israeli universities—calls that come from a minority and are generally rejected, but which are voiced again and again.

And what about organizations dedicated to civil liberties? To the right to fair trial? To abolishing the death penalty? To fighting slavery? Do they recommend boycotts of Saudi Arabia or Syria? Not at all. They're too busy criticizing Israel. Do international organizations for children worry about inciting children or about using them as live bombs and human shields? Not really, if we judge by the frequency of their denunciations of Israel.

But the biggest orgy of hypocrisy and hatred was the 2001 international conference on (please read carefully) "trafficking in women and children, migration and discrimination, gender and racial discrimination, racism against indigenous peoples, and protection of minority rights." The conference was sponsored and organized by the UN and took place in Durban, South Africa, with thousands of participants attending. From the title itself, it should be obvious to the discriminating reader that the number one target of the "international conference" was the state of Israel. If that wasn't clear to you, read the resolutions, most of which were prepared during a preliminary meeting held (you guessed it) in the enlightened city of Tehran. Not only was Israel accused of every crime on earth, but the conference participants declared that anti-Semitism was not (repeat, *not*) a form of discrimination.

No country other than Israel was explicitly accused of anything, or even named, in the Durban resolutions. Gender discrimination? Has anyone heard of such a thing in the Arab world? Not in Durban. (In fact, the word *Israel* itself was never mentioned, either: The international wisdom of the Tehran attendees preferred terms such as "Historic Palestine" or "The Zionist Entity.")

This entire episode could have been an odd curiosity, if it hadn't unfolded to the applause of hundreds of nongovernmental organizations (NGOs) from all continents, almost none of which walked out in protest. Many of these organizations have the illusion that they represent "tomorrow's thinking," but in truth they are more backward than the nineteenth-century colonialists.

In following the reports from this conference, I understood, for the first time in my life, how it must have felt to be a Jew in Germany in the 1930s. The intensity of the venom, the lies, and the hatred were truly amazing. They were led by the worst people, representing the most backward regimes of the world, funding terrorist organizations, trading in women and children, but preaching to Israel and to the Jews. They were happily supported, actively or passively, by every avant-garde NGO in the Western world. Shocked non-Jewish observers at the conference commented that if a resolution to send all Jews to concentration camps were proposed in the prevailing atmosphere, it might actually have been approved. Whether this is an exaggeration, I am not sure. But it was an unbelievable festival of hatred, fully sponsored by the United Nations.

Let us assume, for a moment, without evidence and without proof, that Israel is guilty of serious mistakes. Let us assume, although it is simply not true, that its response to Palestinian terror has been too harsh. Is Israel really the worst offender on this earth? Has it never been attacked by anyone? Did it just wake up one morning and started shooting in all directions? Has anyone heard of the attempts to destroy Israel? Is Israel truly worse than those who have killed Kurds with chemical weapons and massacred blacks in Sudan? Is it worse than the many dictatorial regimes in this world? Is it worse than those who finance and support airplane hijackers? Than countries who do not allow women to go to school? Who have no judicial system? Who have child labor and slavery? Who pollute the world in every possible way, without regard to the consequences?

Something is very sick with the European extreme Left that it spends so much energy attacking Israel, without ever protesting any of the true evils coming from the Middle East. Is it because of blind hatred toward America, who is considered a friend of Israel? Is it because of an insanely romantic view of the Arab world as a bunch of harmless camels riding into the sunset in the desert? Is it because of lingering guilt over past colonialism? Is it just absolute naïveté and ignorance, believing vicious propaganda and slanted media reports? Is it a desire to side with the "underdog" (with a "slight" error of 180 degrees)? Is it all of the above? Or, God forbid, is it because Israel is the home of the Jews? I honestly do not know the source of this obvious obsession, although I wish I did.

Something is equally wrong with the naive young quasi-idealistic people in the college campuses of North America, who are unknowingly supporting an attempt to exterminate millions of Jews, when they campaign for boycotting Israel. Are they just incited by the Arab propaganda machine in the campuses, without knowing any of the facts? Do they really believe that Israel is the worst thing on the face of the earth? Do they understand that, if Israel ceased to exist, a second Holocaust would occur in the Middle East? Would they then march in mild protest while the mass graves were being dug?

I am sure that neither Austria's Jeorg Haider nor America's Pat Buchanan was enamored with the Durban conference, infested as it was by denizens of the far Left. And yet I am equally sure that each would have been more than willing to add their signatures to each of its anti-Israeli resolutions. Food for thought.

—16—

IGNORANCE AND APATHY

The defensive posture of the Western world turns Islamic terror into the best investment ever. A small low-cost group of ruthless people can cause enormous financial damage, which most people accept as if it were a natural disaster.

It is the peak of the summer travel season. One hundred people are standing in line for the security check at the airport. The line moves slowly. The screening process lasts forever. *Take off your shoes. Remove your laptop. Put your keys and cell phone in the box. Remove your jacket. It's still beeping? Maybe it's your belt. Okay, now put on your shoes. Return your laptop. Make sure you haven't taken someone else's cell phone. Don't forget your keys. You made it. Bon voyage!*

For some reason, there's no clear big sign over the machines to remind everyone of the characters to whom we owe all this trouble. Travelers seem to accept it all very peacefully. The cost to the world economy has been enormous, but those who brought it about have never been made to pay.

Here's what happens when you arrive in the United States from abroad: Passport check. Visa check. New photograph taken. Fingerprints taken. It's the same procedure used to process criminals before they're admitted to jail. On every pack of cigarettes we are informed what it is that causes cancer and heart disease. Shouldn't we be reminded in the airports who is responsible for this new burden?

The entire world is growing used to the madness of the antiterror lifestyle. Israelis have lived with it for decades. Back in the days when everybody, including citizens of all the terrorist countries, could arrive at any airport just thirty minutes before takeoff and reach their terminal without ever having to pass through a security check, flights to and from Israel required a two-hour advance check-in and all passengers were segregated from the rest of humanity as if they had some dangerous communicable disease. This attracted no interest from any other countries. There were never any announcements that this was a collective punishment of the victims, while the culprits enjoyed the comfort of unchecked travel.

It is very interesting that the idea of "profiling" certain suspicious groups of passengers is deeply resented by civil liberties organizations, especially when it relates to Arab passengers. The fact that, for years, passengers to Israel were the only ones searched and segregated has never raised an eyebrow in these organizations. The same logic that claims that all passengers should be searched equally, to avoid discriminating certain ethnic groups, should long since have mandated that flights to all destinations should be searched equally—at least all flights to Tehran, Baghdad, Damascus, and Tripoli. Yet somehow "profiling" passengers to Israel as suspicious was more acceptable than "profiling" people from certain other countries.

For decades, ever since a Palestinian woman killed several people by leaving a bomb in a movie theater in Jerusalem, bags and purses are searched in all Israeli public places, especially theaters (coming soon to a theater near you!). But such measures would never have been necessary in the first place, if those responsible for such events had been immediately excluded from the world community, rather than embraced by many world leaders.

These security measures are understandable. We should all be careful and vigilant in safeguarding our families and our public spaces.

But isn't it remarkable that we seem to be accepting them so easily? Isn't there something wrong with a society that agrees to be harassed in such a way without protest, without pushing more forcefully to get at the root of the problem? Could all of this have been avoided?

It is absolutely clear that if the Western world had blocked flights to any country that accepted hijacked planes or refused to extradite hijackers after the first Palestinian hijacking to Algeria in 1968, we would never have seen the events of September 11. But for years it was only flights to Israel that were threatened, and no one got very excited about it. The world is now paying the price. For years, it was only synagogues that were being attacked by terrorists. Not many people cared. Now it has moved on to include Christian churches in Iraq, Pakistan, and Bethlehem. For years, terrorists have been shelling Israeli towns, houses, schools, kindergartens, and shopping centers near the northern border and the Gaza border. This rarely gets covered in the international media; the world has grown tired of the same old story. Why bother? But sooner or later primitive missiles will be launched elsewhere, in other parts of the world, against civilian planes, cars, or residential neighborhoods and everybody will wake up. It would not be difficult at all for terrorists to launch such missiles from a backyard in Paris into the Louvre, to punish the French government for its denunciations of anti-Semitism or for its law against head scarves.

Almost every form of terror the world knows today, from suicide murder to airplane hijacking, from attacking places of worship to abducting people and executing them, from detonating car bombs in crowded places to taking children as hostages in a school, has been tried for years on Israel. And world reaction has been, at best, "evenhanded," and at worst has involved denunciations of Israel. The terrorists have learned that such acts are acceptable and easily forgiven. They have also learned that the affluent world is not willing to fight for its ideas and is often more eager to surrender to blackmail than to insist on principles.

It is so difficult to look ahead and anticipate the trouble before it comes. The world wastes little time thanking the one who prevents a fire; only the one who extinguishes it gets the medals. There is a natural tendency to say: "This is terrible, but it can't happen here." Well, September 11 in New York and Washington and March 11 in Madrid say otherwise. By the same token, it is easy to hope that everything can be settled by discussions and reasoning. Not with these people.

All of this is quite clear to anyone who has spent even a minimal amount of time analyzing the situation. Yet most of the general public, as well as its political leaders—who usually follow the public rather than leading it—display an amazing level of apathy and ignorance on the subject. If the world cannot be wise before the fact, at least after the fact it should act upon the wisdom it has so painfully earned.

A total international quarantine on any country harboring terrorists, financing them, dispatching them, or even tolerating them would put an end to the vast majority of such acts. It is not too late to enact such a ban—and, indeed, it is shortsighted to do the opposite, to negotiate and trade with such countries. The price of appeasement, in lives and in economic damage, will definitely exceed any immediate loss that might arise from excluding these countries from the family of nations. It is clear that such acts can only be taken with a total consensus, not a majority, of the free world. One day, we can hope, such a consensus will emerge, and that day will be the turning point in the war on terror. But every day that passes without such steps increases the terrible cost to humanity.

It is very tempting for the French, the Germans, and others to think,"The Americans and a few allies are fighting the terrorists. We might as well enjoy some business with them while the Americans beat the hell out of them and we sit and doubt the necessity of it." Yet the terrorists will never succeed in restraining themselves, and sooner or later they will attack the French, the Germans, and all the others. The world owes much to this tendency of power-hungry madmen. If Saddam had not invaded Kuwait, today he might be the proud owner of a host of nuclear weapons. If Hitler had been satisfied with western and eastern Europe, and not set his sights on the Soviet Union, French children today might be singing "Deutschland Uber Alles."

Affluence and peace and quiet are the parents of shortsightedness, submission, ignorance, and apathy. In a local election in the United States, in which only 30 percent of the public bothered to vote, a TV interviewer asked someone: "What do you think about the ignorance and the apathy of the American voters?" "I don't know and I don't care," was the quick answer. Unfortunately, this old story is equally applicable to the issue of reacting to terror. The public doesn't seem to care. It accepts the daily intrusion of the security measures without asking who is causing them. Every single news broadcast brings stories about Islamic terror in all corners of the world. Most Europeans and Americans treat it as if it were the latest inevitable tropical storm. Even the abduction and the killing of idealistic, but naive, Western aid workers in Iraq raises only mild indignation. Europeans doubt the need of severe measures, because it's always easier to do nothing. Instead of asking every day: "How can this be reversed?" we hear voices who doubt that the terror threat is real. It is time to wake up.

PART III

THE PERSISTENT LIES

~17~

THE SUPERFICIAL VILLAGE

If TV broadcasts during World War II had only shown the suffering of the citizens of Dresden, Hitler would have been very popular in the salons of New York and Paris.

In the streets of a village in Globania, several sacred cows are wandering around. No one would dare to touch them, at least not for the time being. Actually, they should never be touched, as long as they do not bring a catastrophe upon the inhabitants. But if someone is pulling a submachine gun, standing behind one of these cows, and starts killing people, he should be stopped with force, even if this should hurt one of the cows.

Freedom of religion is, and must be, sacred in the democratic parts of the village. It includes the freedom to be an atheist, and the freedom to practice a religion other than the dominant religion in a particular neighborhood. It does not include the right to use religious preaching for racist incitement, to call for the murder of women and children, or to encourage suicide murders. Nor does it protect the right of religious people to preach for the destruction of entire nations.

Freedom of the press, including the electronic media, is also sacred. It includes the right of the press to be inaccurate and even dead wrong, subject to certain limitations concerning deliberate and harmful defamation. Every free country has its own mild limitations on free speech. In some countries, racial incitement is illegal. There are varying limitations on subjects like child pornography, on one hand, and information endangering the security of the state at times of war, on the other.

In Globania, the rules are much less clear. In some areas, the sacred cows are respected and are not touched. In others, the cows are slaughtered without a second thought. Here the analogy stops. The real sacred cows are heavy. They are "hardware." A sacred cow in one country is unlikely to be physically transported to another part of the world, and it cannot leave its smelly products on the streets of another region. But the proverbial sacred cows named "freedom of the press" and "freedom of religion" are, essentially, forms of software. They are bytes of information that can be transmitted around the globe in less than a second.

If all of Globania followed the same rules, we could easily live with them. If each part of Globania had its own set of rules, but were almost disconnected from one another, as it has been for centuries, the arrangement would be tenable, if not ideal. What cannot work, and does not work, is a situation in which racial incitement is forbidden in Germany, but beamed into it from Qatar or Lebanon.

The combination of freedom of religion and freedom of the media, as practiced in the free world, is a lethal instrument in the hands of the Islamic terrorists and their powerful backers. Their incitement is transmitted by sacredly protected media, using sacredly protected religious preaching and messages. Wave after wave of hatred against America, against the Western world, against Christianity and Judaism, and against Israel is freely propagated, under the pretense of religious statements, using printed and electronic media that no one would even consider blocking.

The modern world is complex, and growing more so every day. Many issues require a perspective of decades, especially when it comes to matters of education, science, religious evolution, or globalization. Many news items have a complex background, without which it is impossible to understand what has happened. At the same time, the sound bite rules the world. We view a thirty-second report about an event happening in some far-off locale, within the context of a culture and politics about which we know next to nothing. The choice of clip is not motivated by trying to present a coherent report. It is, at best, motivated by the desire to enhance viewer interest and ratings. It may well be a misleading choice because of the ignorance of the reporter or the news editor, or because he or she was misled by someone without realizing it. At worst—as happens every day—the clip is selected with a clear intent to harm someone. It is amazingly easy to do it, without explicitly lying.

Regardless of terrorism, fundamentalism, and the raging storm, this is a very dangerous situation. It has been anticipated by many, and for many years. All of these dangers have materialized just as they were foreseen, sometimes exceeding the worst fears. Books have been written about the phenomena, lectures and courses are given with numbing regularity, but still there is no clear solution for the problem.

Enter the age of interactive media. We can now obtain instant public feedback to the slanted or superficial news item over the Internet, and in some newspapers and TV stations. But more, and worse, is coming. By showing one or two thirty-second segments, which are technically true but tell half or less than half of a story, you can destroy the name of a person, a company, or any other entity, economic or political. You may then receive an immediate public vote of confidence in your judgment, based on your ignorant, careless, or deliberately false reporting, in answer to a question formulated in an unfair way. You are performing the precise electronic equivalent of a mob in the street who hears a shout: "Get that black man who raped the little white girl!" upon which the suspect is literally torn to pieces or hanged in the city square, with no chance to defend himself. In short, this is the electronic version of lynching.

Yes, every civilized country has checks and balances, and every respectable news organization would try to avoid such situations. But this depends on the sources of information and on the freedom of reporting from distant countries, which have no freedom of speech or freedom of the press. And in such countries, the phrase "respectable news organization" has an entirely different meaning.

Three major factors play into the hands of terrorist networks and their supporters, in the battle for the attention and sympathy of the uninformed European or American, who is used to believing, at least approximately, what his news media are saying.

The first factor is the freedom of controlled, racist news organizations, whether satellite TV channels or quasi-news websites, to spread their gospel all over the world, without checks and balances. They can lie permanently and repeatedly, in words and in pictures, without anyone exposing them. If British or Swedish news media repeatedly declared, without the slightest evidence, that a British citizen or Swedish organization has performed multiple murders or even genocide, there would be legal and moral ways of dealing with the situation. Yet when Arab satellite TV channels beam their continuous stream of lies and defamation to the Arabic-speaking minorities in France, Belgium, and the United States, no one can stop them. Indeed, most who might want to stop them don't watch their broadcasts or even understand their language. In the meantime, an ugly wave of hatred and fanaticism is spreading like fire among European Muslims, whose majority has always been traditionally peaceful and law-abiding.

The second issue is the total practical dependence of Western media correspondents on local talent. The correspondents of an Italian or a Spanish TV network in Iraq, Iran, Syria, Lebanon, or the Palestinian areas, cannot move freely. They can only report from places where they are allowed to travel, driven by local drivers and collecting information through local interpreters. Their hosts may influence whom they select to be interviewed, and may not even be able to conduct the interviews directly. The correspondents, and especially the people who they interview, are often intimidated by silent, stern-looking onlookers, whose role is unstated yet clear. All along the way they are at the mercy of their local guides, often driven through dangerous areas by local drivers who know how to avoid scenes the local interests don't want exposed to the wider world; in the same vein, they often rely on local camera-men who know to avoid certain pictures and angles.

All of these may sound like trivial technical matters, but in prac-tice they often lead to totally distorted reporting, with or without the acquiescence of the Western reporter. Shooting the same scene from a different angle can make an enormous difference, as every TV corre-spondent knows very well. Zooming in on ten loud demonstrators in a huge empty square gives a completely different news item than show-ing the entire square. Yet the correspondent cannot always control the cameraman, who may be working under fire and doing whatever his own nationalistic interest dictates to him.

The third issue is the fear factor. Reporting from the field, a corre-spondent can be subject to direct intimidation—from threats of abduc-tion and decapitation, not unknown in certain countries, to the much more subtle, but much more practical, practice of hinting that access to support and information will be denied to the "unfriendly corre-spondent." In Iraq, Western journalists are often abducted by the ter-rorists. In the Palestinian areas, terror reigns just as surely when it comes to journalists.

In the early months of the latest Palestinian wave of terror, an Ital-ian TV crew experienced this terror firsthand. They shot footage of a bloody lynching in which two Israeli soldiers who took a wrong turn driving their private car were ruthlessly murdered. Their bodies were torn into pieces by a Palestinian mob with the active help of the Pales-tinian police, who proudly displayed their hands dipped in the blood of the victims. The Italian TV network was warned by Palestinian author-ities never to broadcast these pictures; the crew was hastily returned to Italy in order to protect their lives, and the film was never shown in Italy. Its very existence became a secret. It was finally smuggled some-how to Israeli TV, but was never shown in Europe. Since then, most Italian TV reports from the Palestinian areas have been openly anti-Israeli. The reason is obvious: fear for the lives of the crews.

The terror campaign against "unfriendly" journalists has been ap-parent since the civil war in Lebanon, and during the reports from

Baghdad during the 1991 Gulf War. But the present level of intimidation far outstrips anything known in the past. Here and there, news organizations like Reuters and CNN have admitted to being influenced by threats, but most media outlets refuse to admit the obvious.

The major networks generally respond to these factors in two ways—both of which should be unacceptable, but are widely practiced. One is to use correspondents who speak the local language and are local inhabitants. An Arab correspondent of CNN, covering Palestinian terror or events in Iraq, may have more access to certain information than an American, but the resulting news coverage offered to tens of millions of people around the world is—to understate the case—not exactly unbiased.

A more frequent approach, practiced mostly by the printed media, is to solve the problem by reporting all the vicious lies, well aware that they *are* lies, always carefully quoting the Iranian or Palestinian source and never reporting the facts that reveal the blatant lie. Quoting sources this way allows the print media to claim that they're being responsible, objective journalists. But professional journalism also demands that when you hear one side lying and you know this for a fact, you report it to your audience.

Open any American newspaper, and you may come across a statement attributed to "UN personnel" in Gaza, blasting some Israeli policy or action. Sounds official enough, no? Yet what the correspondent isn't telling you is that the quoted "UN personnel" is a Palestinian. (The United Nations has admitted to employing members of Hamas in Gaza.) Again, without quite lying, the newspaper has managed to leave a crucial part of the truth "neglected."

The average reader is not paying attention to the fine print. If he reads every day that the Israelis stop ambulances at checkpoints, risking the lives of the sick and wounded, and that this was announced by the Palestinian medical services, he does not know that the same medical services have arranged for an explosive suicide belt to be hidden beneath a three-year-old child on the stretcher in an ambulance, and have hidden terrorists in hospital beds. The Western correspondent knows it, but chooses not to remind anyone. He has three excuses for not including the crucial background fact: *It's yesterday's news; I shouldn't make the locals angry; it is too long a story to get across in a short news report.*

Another interesting game is to report on yet another suicide murder in Iraq, where twenty-five Iraqis are indiscriminately murdered, while on the screen you see again and again the same American tank moving in the same street of an Iraqi city, far from the bloody scene of the suicide. The picture is authentic. The text is correct. But they are unrelated to each other and create an impression that wasn't intended by the correspondent in the field—and is fundamentally wrong.

Every beginning journalist knows the ancient story about the Italian cardinal who landed in New York, having been warned by his aides to be cautious with the aggressive American press. As he emerged from the airplane, he was asked: "Eminence, what are your views about the gay community in New York?" Trying to gain time and to think, he mumbled quietly "Is there a gay community in New York?" The banner headline of the evening newspapers was accurate: "The Cardinal's first question, upon landing: Is there a gay community in New York?"

A substantial portion of the international news reporting from the Middle East is no more reliable or objective than that headline. One needn't look hard for examples. They appear in almost every single issue of every single newspaper in Europe and the United States.

—18—

WORDS KILL

Bombs take hours or days to reach every corner of the earth.
Words arrive instantly and kill more people. They are a weapon
of mass destruction.

Islamic terrorists hijack planes. They kidnap journalists. They murder by suicide. They decapitate victims. They desecrate holy places. They shoot missiles and shells into civilian areas. They deliberately murder children and old people. They hold hostages. They blow up buses, trains, nightclubs, shopping malls, synagogues, churches, schools. They do so in all corners of the world.

In all of their endeavors, the terrorists use two major types of weapons. The first is "conventional": explosives, bombs, grenades, firearms, missiles, shells. But the second major weapon is widely ignored, and it is no less lethal. It is words: lies, lies, and lies, amplified by controlled or manipulated global media. These deliberate, systematic lies, repeated until they have the ring of truth, are all the more dangerous for their apparent harmlessness.

Words can be deadly. They kill people. It is often said that politicians, diplomats, and even lawyers and businesspeople must sometimes lie as part of their professional life. But the norms of politics and diplomacy are childish when compared with the level of incitement and deliberate fabrication in the region we are talking about. An incredible number of people in the Arab world believe that September 11 never happened, or was an American provocation or, better yet, a Jewish plot.

Words are the infrastructure of the Jihad. The lies are produced by the terrorists, by their chiefs, by their supporters, and by national leaders who behave in an ambiguous way, oscillating between a reluctant acceptance of terrorism and a mild applause. The lies give legitimacy to the acts. They help recruit new terrorists. They mislead the world into believing that the terrorists may have some valid causes, or that certain senseless murders can be partly justified.

The lies start at the level of simple incorrect facts, and escalate into totally baseless statements about genocide, war crimes, apartheid and the like. They cover the past, the present, and the future. When these are repeated again and again, without the slightest component of truth or the least evidence, good honest naive people begin to believe them. New anti-American feelings are fueled. Traditional anti-Semitic movements flourish. Suicide candidates join the ranks. Innocent Europeans are tempted into boycotts, demonstrations, and petitions—and against whom? Against the *victims* of terror. The words provide an emotional infrastructure for the atrocities that follow. It was the Nazi propaganda guru, Joseph Goebbels, who said that if you repeated a lie often enough, people would believe it. He is now being outperformed by his successors.

You may still remember Saddam Hussein's minister of information, Mohammed Saeed al-Sahaf, and the press conferences he gave even after U.S. forces were already inside Baghdad. Disinformation in time of war is an accepted tactic. But to make such preposterous statements, day after day, without even being ridiculed in your own milieu, can only happen in this region. Eventually, al-Sahaf became a popular icon as a court jester, but this didn't stop some allegedly respectable newspapers from giving him equal time. It also doesn't prevent the Western press from giving credence, even now, to similar liars. After all, if you want to be an anti-Semite, there are subtle ways of doing it. You don't have to claim the Holocaust never happened, or that the Jewish temple in Jerusalem never existed. But millions of Muslims are told by their leaders that this is the case—and other statements made by those same leaders are regularly reported in the Western press as if they could be true.

An incredible game of terminology is going on. The suicide perpetrators of September 11 were clearly terrorists. So was the suicide bomber who blew himself up in the 2001 Passover Seder, killing twenty-seven elderly people. Yet according to all European media and most American media, he was a Palestinian "activist."

A European delegation came to visit the late Yasir Arafat in Ramallah, led by a well-known Frenchman who had repeatedly claimed on French TV that September 11 was an American plot. He and several members of his group participated in violent antiglobalization riots in various places in Europe. Some members of the delegation were known right-wing European extremists, others from the far Left; they were unified, as always, by that hatred of Jews that has so long united fascists and communists. All reports on this delegation referred to them as "peace activists." Even the rascals themselves did not dare to refer to themselves as such; they called themselves a "Palestinian solidarity delegation." But for a couple of days we could watch and hear, again and again, on all Western TV stations, how Arafat kissed a "peace activist" on the forehead.

An anti-American demonstration in Berlin, carrying banners supporting Saddam's regime and featuring three-year-old children dressed as suicide murderers, was defined by the press and by political leaders as a "peace demonstration." You may support or oppose the Iraq War, but to refer to fans of Saddam, Arafat, or bin Laden as peace activists is a bit too much.

Can it be that the journalists knew who these people were and who financed them, and simply lied to the viewers? Did they never bother to do the minimal research it would have taken to find out? Did they deliberately choose to ignore the reports telling them exactly who these groups were? Only the "professional, objective world press" knows the answer. But words like these can kill by the atmosphere they create, by the acceptance they induce, and by encouraging people who are truly peaceloving to join the ranks of the pro-terrorist groups.

It happens daily that the same people who finance, arm, and dispatch suicide murderers then turn and condemn the act in English for Western TV cameras, talking to a world audience that may actually believe them. It occurs daily that the same leader makes one statement to his people in Arabic, and then takes the opposite position in English for the rest of the world. Arab TV's efforts to incite violence, and their airing of horrific pictures of mutilated bodies, has become a powerful weapon of those who lie, distort, and wish to destroy everything in their path. Little children are raised on a diet of deep hatred for their enemies and admiration of so-called martyrs, and the Western world never notices because its own TV sets are tuned to soap operas and so-called "reality TV." I recommend that everyone take a few minutes one day to watch Al Jazeera—even those who don't understand Arabic. It is an eye-opening experience.

But Al Jazeera is child's play compared to Al-Manar, the Hizbullah TV station, which is beamed into most European countries and the entire Middle East. The insane lies of Al-Manar include claims that Israel is spreading contagious diseases and deadly viruses in the Arab world; that Israel is producing toy dolls stuffed with explosives to kill Arab children; and other fantasies of a kind only a truly sick mind could invent. The satellites that transmit these broadcasts are owned by Europeans and Saudis. Have they even considered blocking them?

There are other games of language afoot, of course. The actual murderer is called "the military wing;" the one who pays him, equips him, and sends him is called "the political wing;" and the head of the operation is called the "spiritual leader." This terminology is obviously intended to provide the real terror chiefs with deniability and protection. There are numerous other examples of such Orwellian nomenclature, used every day by the terror chiefs and all too often adopted by the Western media.

A special category of lethal words are the great taboos: *Racism, genocide, war crimes, apartheid, holocaust, and ethnic cleansing.* The method is simple. Just use these words again and again, assigning them to the people you would like to murder and eliminate. The reality does not matter. If enough people hear again and again that El Salvador is performing genocide against Indonesia, enough people will automatically associate the name El Salvador with genocide. This sounds unbelievable, but it does work. The only Western nation that has willingly accepted black immigrants with no education and low health standards is Israel, which made an enormous effort to absorb the Ethiopian Jews. This does not stop the Arabs from referring to it as a racist state. These are the same Arabs who murdered the black population in Sudan, who historically were the leading slave traders between Africa and America, and who treat foreign workers in the Gulf states as second-class citizens. All of this doesn't matter, not if you repeat your lies every day.

The fence or wall erected by Israel against suicide murderers has been labeled by the truthful Arafat as "the apartheid wall." It was a very clever tactical move. South Africa's hated apartheid regime was, rightfully, a symbol of injustice for millions of decent people around the world. Why not turn these people into anti-Semites by creating an equation between Israel and apartheid? The system of apartheid was a white minority regime that denied the majority population its right to vote, and all other civil rights, through legislation that discriminated among people by their color and separated the races. How is this related to the Jewish majority in Israel who, of course, gave the Arab minority the right to vote and all other civil rights? Perhaps the French occupation forces in Germany, after World War II, were also guilty of apartheid, not to speak of the current French attitude toward its own Muslim minority? No, none of these matter; just repeat the words *Israel* and *apartheid* twenty times a day, and you'll get boycotts, demonstrations, and hate. The trick even works on French ambassadors, who happily repeat this unholy marriage of words—and yet pretend to be offended if they are accused of anti-Semitism. In the meantime, the suicide murderers still stride into supermarkets. Why not? The world has done nothing to stop them.

There are frequent complaints about the treatment of the Arab minority in Israel. It is not easy to be a member of such a minority. But Belgium, France, and the Netherlands also have substantial Arab minorities. It would be interesting to compare indicators such as education level, life expectancy, the number of university students, the number of judges and police officers, average income, and other conditions under which the Arab minorities live in each of these countries. I am convinced that in most, if not all, of these the conditions in Israel are the best among all these countries, even though the Arab world wants to destroy Israel rather than France or Belgium. Has anyone talked about apartheid in France? Certainly not the French ambassador, who talks about Israel and its "apartheid."

Denying that the Holocaust happened is not a frivolous opinion hazarded by a few in the Arab world. It is printed as truth in government newspapers in the most "moderate" Arab countries—including Egypt, which has diplomatic relations and a peace agreement with Israel, and Saudi Arabia, the great friend of the United States. Why does it matter? Among other reasons, because any other statement made by these governments should thus be considered suspect at best.

At any given time, the Americans could slaughter any number of Iraqis, Syrians, or Afghanis at will. Of course, they do not; they would never even think about it. Israel can annihilate any Palestinian city, village, or camp, if it wants to. Of course, it does not. But innocent civilians are killed, from time to time, in the war against the terrorists. To refer to this as genocide, when a million people are murdered by the Arabs in Sudan, requires unbelievable chutzpah. Israel does not even have a death penalty; even when the worst Arab multiple murderers are caught alive, they are never executed.

Consider what the news from the Middle East must look like through the eyes of an intelligent, reasonably educated person in America, the Far East, or Europe, with no firsthand knowledge of Middle East history or geography. Military acts, they learn, are constantly being performed by people described as "activists," "militants," or "fighters." These acts are gallantly condemned by Arab leaders from a distance, but their targets are people somehow guilty of genocide and apartheid, war crimes and racism. The fighters who commit the acts enjoy the support of peace activists and represent masses of poor people who have been suppressed for years. This portrait is painted daily, and not only by Al Jazeera. It comes from CNN, BBC, and most European, Japanese, and Chinese networks. After steady exposure to that story for years, how hard would it be to conclude that the world would be a much better place if all the Jews were eliminated?

And consider this one additional sobering fact: More than half the population of the Arab world is under the age of twenty—the most impressionable age there is. With the lies they consume daily, is there any way to prevent the next two generations from being possessed by blind hatred and terror?

—19—

PICTURES LIE

A picture is better than a thousand words. A misleading picture is worse than a thousand lies.

Pictures can lie, even when they are authentic. A news item about a brutal rapist and murderer, accompanied only by a heartbreaking photograph of his poor old crying mother after hearing his sentence, is a lie, even if both the picture and the text are truthful. A report on the Olympic Games that shows only pictures of dirty toilets in the Olympic Stadium at the end of the competition conveys a totally false message about the games. Even if the article calls the Olympic Games a smashing success, and mentions in passing that dirty toilets were a minor problem, the viewer is likely to remember only the unpleasant visual. When one hundred thousand people demonstrate somewhere for some cause, and amid these thousands a group of twenty opponents carries banners with the opposite position, even the most responsible written coverage of the event can be falsified if it's accompanied only by a big close-up photo of the small renegade group. Both the picture and the text will be authentic, but the result will be a serious lie. (I did not invent this last example. It happened in a very distinguished American newspaper.)

Global terrorism and its photographic coverage offer opportunities for distortion that are unmatched by any previous war. The asymmetry of the conflict almost invites such reporting. You cannot take pictures of the terrorist who plans to kill the children, before or during the act. But you can show the pre-planned video in which he blasts the American criminals, the Russian butchers, or the Zionist murderers. You cannot catch a snapshot of the terrorists launching a missile into a residential neighborhood and murdering innocent civilians, but you can later show army and police units looking for the terrorists among dilapidated houses and poor areas, which appear to be violated by the mere picture of a Jeep driving through them. Not that the terrorists are poor. Their leaders are affluent, but the actual murderers will always hide in such places, even though they are usually well paid for their "work."

Here is our own random album of such lying pictures from the eye of the storm:

During the first few months of the current Palestinian terror wave, children were being sent to throw stones and rocks at the Israeli soldiers, with adults often standing behind them and shooting at the soldiers with live ammunition. The Israeli army was trying to cope with the children using tear gas, but had to shoot back at the armed adults. As the world watched on the news every evening, Israeli soldiers in vehicles and tanks were seen shooting at children throwing stones. Almost every day one or more Israeli soldiers were killed by Palestinian gunmen, but for months not one international viewer saw a single Palestinian shooting. No viewer, no correspondent, and no news editor asked himself who was killing the soldiers, if only harmless stones were being thrown. The cameramen on the scene were all Palestinians, carefully choosing angles showing the children and the Israeli soldiers, never the hidden shooting terrorists. Not one word was said about this, and when the Israeli government complained bitterly to the media, its arguments were disregarded as propaganda.

For weeks and weeks, every image seen on the screen was authentic. Yet the overall emerging picture was a blatant lie. In 2004, the terrorists even "improved" their technique. They sent the children to throw stones at tanks, knowing that the Israelis would avoid shooting at them; the adults behind them were now equipped with handheld anti-tank weapons, capable of penetrating the armor and killing the crew.

The headline? "Breaking news: Children fighting tanks."

The *International Herald Tribune* is the favorite newspaper of most English-speaking world travelers. For months and months, every news report from the Middle East on its pages was accompanied by photographs of poor, crying Palestinian children or destroyed Palestinian houses. Often, the news item was the suicide murder of a dozen Israeli women, children, and old people, but the accompanying photograph almost always depicted the "cruelty" of the Israelis. On other days, when nothing special was reported from the Middle East, or when the only Middle East news came from the United Nations or Washington, the front page still carried the daily photo of a crying Palestinian woman surrounded by children, or an old Palestinian man facing an Israeli soldier. What photo editor made this judgment, why he or she did so, and why the newspaper accepted it, is a mystery to me. But a picture is stronger than a thousand words.

The terrorists often use houses and apartments of normal non-combatant Palestinians in order to shoot at, or to shell, Israeli positions or Israeli civilian neighborhoods. They evacuate their own people from their houses at night to use them as staging grounds, sometimes allowing them to come back during the day. This has been done in the town of Beth Jallah, a suburb of Bethlehem, from which Jewish neighborhoods of Jerusalem were attacked; in Raffah in the Gaza strip, where tunnels were dug into Egypt and the Israeli garrison was attacked daily; and in northern Gaza, where dozens of missiles have been fired into Israeli towns and villages from crowded Palestinian neighborhoods.

This strategy is a real winner. It forces Israel to decide whether to accept the firing without any response or to attack and destroy the houses. In the first case, Israelis are bound to be killed with no recourse. They are sitting ducks. In the latter case, when fire is returned and the house is destroyed or damaged, with no innocent civilians anywhere near it, the real theatrical show begins. As soon as morning comes, the Palestinian inhabitants, who were driven out of their houses earlier by the terrorists, are brought back just in time for the foreign TV crews to photograph them among the ruins of their houses. The entire world sees the heartbreaking scenes of children finding their toys in the rubble, unaware that these children were unceremoniously thrown out of their own houses earlier by their own "friends," and their rooms used as shooting positions for the purpose of killing other children.

The Arab media has also launched a concerted campaign of showing fragments of dead bodies on all Arab TV stations. The worst such case occurred in 2001, when Palestinians in Gaza planted a huge land mine on a path where they were expecting Israeli vehicles to pass. A Palestinian woman and her four children, riding a donkey cart, hit the Palestinian mine. Tragically, all were killed. The Arab stations repeatedly showed the shattered bodies of the children, claiming that the Israelis murdered them. How many suicide bombers were inspired to join the terrorists' ranks as a result? Who reported this to the Western world?

Another example of this game happened around the same time, when the worst murderers in Bethlehem, responsible for a large number of suicide attacks and for murdering numerous Israeli civilians, children, women, and the elderly, used their weapons to get into the Nativity Church. They shot open the locks on the church doors and took forty priests and nuns as hostages. The Israeli army surrounded the church, but did not storm it. For days we heard the hostage priests saying that the terrorists had asked for asylum and laid down their weapons—a clear lie, obviously stated under duress. Yet the world media persisted in showing image after image of soldiers and tanks surrounding the church, implying that Israel was attacking the holy site, never explaining that the priests had been taken as hostages in the holy church by the same group. The image of tanks poised to attack the Nativity Church was what most viewers would remember, not the facts—those, and the condemnations of Israel issued by the Vatican.

The wall or fence or barrier erected by Israel to stop suicide murderers is very photogenic. It looks threatening and inhuman. Not as inhuman as a suicide murder with body fragments, heads, and limbs scattered around, but such pictures are never shown with the wall. The wall is also covered, in a few places, by vicious anti-Israeli and anti-Jewish graffiti. So be it. If TV stations cover the issue of the wall itself, it is perfectly reasonable that they show it.

But now there is a new trend. A CNN report about Palestinians training for a swimming competition shows them jogging along the wall, stopping by the graffiti so that we can all read it. A report on the first day of school shows Palestinians walking by the wall. In their coverage of Middle Eastern affairs, European TV stations inevitably show pictures of the wall and its slogans, although they have no connection to events in question. Nor, of course, do they ever explain how many lives have been saved by the wall. The wall has lately replaced the standard ten-second clip of an Israeli tank in the main street of Ramallah, which used to be shown again and again, when any Middle East news was reported.

Another favorite of many TV stations is a clip showing Israeli soldiers at a checkpoint, stopping an ambulance for a security search. Since the beginning of the intifada, the Palestinians have systematically used ambulances to move terrorists, explosives, and weapons—a practice actively supported and managed by certain elements of the Palestinian Red Crescent (the Red Cross equivalent). One young Palestinian woman transported into Jerusalem in a Palestinian ambulance, and allowed to pass at the Israeli checkpoint, proceeded to blow herself up in the center of Jerusalem, killing an eighty-year-old man and wounding dozens. Not one word about the use of the ambulance was published in the Western press. Israel is thus forced to check ambulances carefully—and yet the TV networks persist in showing these images, to suggest how "the Israelis delay the wounded and the sick." In fact, the Palestinians have ushered foreign TV crews to these checkpoints to watch the searching of ambulances. The TV reporters, of course, never mention who brought them to the scene, or why the ambulances are being searched.

The entire medical front, touching the sensitivities of every reasonable Israeli soldier, is also enlisted in the service of the Palestinians, hiding terrorists in hospital beds while they masquerade as patients. One terrorist headquarters was housed in a mental hospital. Terrorists reach checkpoints, pretending to be in need of urgent medical help, loaded with explosives. Most Palestinian doctors are totally shocked by this behavior, but more than a few collaborate with these acts, willingly or unwillingly. For the terrorists, it is a win-win strategy. Sometimes they succeed in smuggling explosives and terrorists, but every time they succeed in showing the TV networks how the cruel Israelis stop ambulances and search hospitals. The pictures are very strong; there is always a stern-looking Palestinian doctor eager to explain the Israelis' heartless cruelty. The TV correspondents know very well what is going on, but they never mention it. If the truth were exposed, it might spoil the pictures.

The height of outrage was reached when Israeli soldiers, at a checkpoint on the road to Jerusalem, stopped an ambulance carrying a father, mother, and their three children, one of them (a three-year-old) on a stretcher. Under the stretcher, the soldiers found a suicide bomber's explosive belt with twelve cylinders of explosives mixed with nails and screws. The driver was delivering it to a suicide murderer to be exploded in Jerusalem, using the child as cover. The representatives of the International Red Cross were invited to witness this, and they lodged a complaint with the Palestinian Red Crescent. Yet not a word about the incident appeared in the Western news media. TV crews arrived at the scene; mysteriously, however, no reports were filed. All we saw were more TV shots of Israeli soldiers stopping ambulances at checkpoints.

These are but a few snapshots from the album. Why are such things allowed to happen? I am not sure. Sometimes it's because these are indeed "good pictures." Other times, perhaps, it proves impossible to explain the context of an event in a single thirty-second news segment. More often, however, it's because local cameramen, drivers, and translators have free rein to influence the way the story is reported and photographed. And because reporters try to please them, hoping to make them into friends and helpful collaborators. One can only hope it's rarely because the reporters themselves are deliberately taking sides—out of conviction or worse.

—20—

THE TRUTH, BUT NOT
THE WHOLE TRUTH

*If a truth is only a selected small part of the whole truth, it may
not be a truth.*

Imagine you are a taxi driver, proverbial or real, in a small town in
Australia or in Korea. You have never left your country, never been
in New York, and never seen an actual big city or a skyscraper. It is
the morning of September 12, 2001. You sit in your taxi, reading your
favorite daily local newspaper while you wait for your first passenger,
and you come across the following news report about yesterday's events:

> Two buildings were destroyed today in New York in what appears to
> have been an attack carried out by unidentified activists. A govern-
> ment spokesman in Washington claimed that several thousand
> people, many in uniform and some civilians, were allegedly killed.
> He blamed the attack on what he described as Arab militants.
> There is no confirmation of the attack from any reliable Arab
> sources. An unconfirmed message received by the Associated Press
> in Damascus, from a previously unknown organization, stated that
> "this was an attack on an American military installation, carried
> out by Saudi citizens as their response to the atrocities performed by

the United States against the Arab Nation over the last 50 years."
Other Islamic sources indicated that the explosions were probably
triggered by the Israeli Mossad to raise anti-Muslim feelings in
America. Sources in Washington are claiming that two commercial
airplanes are missing and that they have been allegedly seen hitting
the two buildings. No firm evidence or remnants of the missing
planes has yet been found around the buildings. An anonymous
caller to the French Press Agency office in Riyadh mentioned the
name of Ahmed Salim as a "martyr who participated in the operation." In Riyadh, Mrs. Salim, identified as the mother of the martyr,
could not hold her tears. "These are tears of joy," she said to her numerous well-wishers. "My son's heroic act will teach the American
murderers a lesson." Mrs. Salim added that her brother has been
jailed in the United States and was falsely accused and sentenced
for multiple murders of children. "My son has avenged his uncle's
cruel fate," she added. Mr. Salim, her husband, has been suffering
from a serious ailment and has been refused treatment by the
American authorities, when he demanded to be flown by them, at
their expense, to a New York hospital. "I am an old man," he said,
exasperated. "Why are the Americans trying to kill me?" A
spokesperson for the Pentagon warned that the United States will
pursue and punish those responsible for the attack.

What did you learn from this report? More than 75 percent of its
text was drawn from Arab sources, offering a combination of veiled allegations, direct accusations, and outright lies. The quotes are probably
authentic. The correspondent probably knew that they were lies, but
chose not to share this with his readers. Every statement attributed to
an American source included the words "claim" and "allegedly." The
report does not clarify who the perpetrators were, and what role the
planes had, if any, in the attacks. Everything is shrouded in doubt. The
terrorists are identified as activists or militants. Even when the American spokesman accuses terrorists, the report refers to "what he described as militants," a word he clearly never uttered. The devastation
and casualties are never described. The fact that uniformed firemen

and policemen died in the attacks gives the correspondent an opening to hint, without saying directly, that this was a military target. The mention of one Saudi man's totally irrelevant ailment helps create a false impression that Americans are generally inconsiderate to human suffering. Mrs. Salim, who could not possibly have been happy that her son had died, probably made her statement through an interpreter, under the watchful eye of someone who brought the journalist to her and never left them alone. None of this, of course, is revealed by the correspondent in his report.

What you, the hypothetical taxi driver, learn from this report is that Americans have been behaving in an atrocious way for years, jailing innocent people and refusing to help the sick. You also learn that some kind of attack has been made by unknown figures, probably on a military target, although the details are not clear. When your first passenger arrives, the details begin to slip slowly from your memory; only the general bad impressions of the United States remain.

This entire story surely sounds, to any reasonable person, like an absolute fabrication. It is. Yet many reports about the Middle East, including those in the world's most prestigious newspapers, reflect the true Israeli-Palestinian situation no better than the above write-up reflects the tragedy of September 11. The technique is the same. The worst murderers are activists or militants, never terrorists or murderers. Every Israeli statement is a "claim" and is "alleged." When an Israeli spokesman refers explicitly to "terrorists," the newspaper replaces the word, even in a quote, with its own "evenhanded" terminology. The event may be the murder of twenty Israelis in a random civilian bus by a suicide attack. If the victims include old people, women, children, and a female soldier who happened to be there, the report will mention "Israeli soldiers and civilians." There will be no description of the severely wounded, the body fragments and the shattered families. But there is always a "human interest" element that gives the name and a description of some Palestinian family, including one or more of the following words: *ailing, refugee, angry, suffering, tearful, victims,* and so on.

If the above words sound angry, it is because they are written by a very angry person. If they sound like an exaggeration, I beg to differ. As a simple test, I submit the first *New York Times* report on the Middle East on the day I am writing this. Chosen at random, it does not describe a very important event. It is just a normal daily report in a respectable American newspaper, which is less anti-Israeli than most European newspapers.

What is the real story? The terrorists in Gaza are doing everything possible to blow up the Israeli checkpoints between Gaza and Israel and between Gaza and Egypt. Their own weapons are smuggled through the tunnels dug from Gaza to Egypt, bypassing the official crossing points. A few weeks before the report, several people were killed in terrorist attacks against some of the border crossing points. A few days before the report in question, a Palestinian woman arrived at one of the Israeli border checkpoints. As she passed through the metal detector, alarms started ringing. She started crying, telling the Israeli security man that she had a platinum replacement piece in her leg and she was on her way to receive treatment in Israel. Unfortunately, the guard was softened by her tears and allowed her to pass. She pulled a string, blew herself up, killing the good-hearted Israeli guard and two others. Israeli intelligence learned that the crossing point between Gaza and Egypt would be the next target. Indeed, a week after the report, a Palestinian arrived at another border point, claiming to have cancer, equipped with (forged) papers and pretending to need medical help in an Israeli hospital. He later testified that he had been tutored in the symptoms of his fictitious ailment, so that he could answer questions. He almost gained access, when it was found that he was carrying a suicide explosive belt. No harm was done, and he was arrested.

The Israeli army decided to close all the crossing points temporarily in order to fortify the security screening posts. While the border checkpoint from Gaza to Egypt was closed, Israel offered Palestinians the option of crossing an Egyptian-Israeli border point, a few kilometers away, entering Israel, and then proceeding back to Gaza. This was a minor detour, not a great inconvenience. The Palestinians authorities refused, using an absurd excuse, and as a result many of their people were stuck in Egypt near the closed border. They were in Egyptian territory, near Egyptian doctors, hospitals, and normal Egyptian medical services. After a couple of weeks' worth of reconstruction, the border crossing was reopened. Nothing really exciting happened, no one died, nothing earthshaking transpired. But here is some of what the *New York Times* reported on August 7, 2004, under the byline of Greg Myre, dateline Jerusalem, Aug. 6:

> Israel opened a border crossing on Friday between the Gaza Strip and Egypt that had been closed for nearly three weeks, allowing most of the more than 2,000 stranded Palestinians to return home. Israel closed the Rafah crossing on July 18, saying it believed that Palestinians were planning to attack the site. Since then, Palestinians who were in Egypt have been unable to return to Gaza.

The report then describes how, while affluent Palestinians waited in Cairo, the other travelers—some of whom were still ailing after medical treatment in Egypt—were cooped up in an uncomfortably hot and inhospitable terminal building on the Egyptian side.

We are then told that a doctor named Khalil Abu Foul from the Palestinian Red Crescent had been allowed to cross from Gaza to Egypt. Abu Foul had "treated the stranded Palestinians for the past two weeks," the piece said. "He said one woman gave birth and two women had miscarriages, while many people suffered from illnesses related to diarrhea and high blood pressure."

And it wasn't only living people who waited, according to the published story. There were also some dead bodies on the way home. The article quotes a man named Abu Muhammad al-Salahiat, describing how his father and aunt had gone to Egypt in search of medical treatment. But when they both apparently died in Cairo, he was forced to wait for the return of their bodies. Al-Salahiat is described as "exasperated," lamenting, "They are both dead. . . . Why won't they let the bodies cross?"

According to the report, "Egypt had called on Israel to reopen the border for aid reasons, and the United States raised the issue."

The *Times* story says that "Israel had offered to allow a limited number of border crossings by Palestinians to pass through a separate crossing along the Israeli-Egyptian border." But it notes that the Palestinian had turned down the offer, calling it "a violation of the existing agreement on the border crossing." According to the newspaper, Israel's offer would have allowed "just 200 Palestinians" per day to cross the border.

The *Times* report closed with a note that one Taghreed El Khodary had contributed reporting from Gaza.

If you think that our fictitious version of an Arab report on September 11 is an exaggeration, read this report carefully.

First, it is clear that much, if not all, of the report comes from an Arab correspondent in Gaza, Mr. El Khodary, even if the name of the *Times'* American correspondent in Jerusalem appears at the top. All the interviews were certainly conducted by El Khodary, as the *Times* should certainly have made clearer in its byline.

Second, the report includes not one word from any Israeli source, except an obscure statement that "it believed the Palestinians were planning to attack the site." The elementary rule of asking the other side for a comment is totally ignored. The reader is never informed exactly what the Israelis said about the incident, and it is clear that they were not approached for a reaction.

Third, there is no mention of the repeated attacks, suicides, killings, failed attempts, and bombings that have occurred at the Gaza border crossings. On the contrary, reports by the same correspondent having anything to do with Temple Mount in Jerusalem always remind us of Sharon's visit there in September 2000—hardly the latest news.

Fourth, given that the Palestinians were stranded in Egypt, it's not at all clear why the Egyptian authorities are not mentioned. Women were giving birth and having miscarriages in Egypt, near Egyptian hospitals, but the writer clearly implies that Israel should be blamed for it. Why aren't the Egyptian medical services even mentioned? Presumably the nearby Egyptian doctors are perfectly capable of treating diarrhea and delivering babies.

Fifth, Israel allowed a Palestinian doctor to cross through the closed crossing point and help the waiting people, even though there must have been ample Egyptian medical help. This is somehow presented as yet another Israeli atrocity, and the thankful doctor is quoted as blaming Israel for all sorts of things.

Sixth, according to the report itself, two thousand Palestinians tried to cross the border in the space of twenty days, meaning an average of one hundred per day. Yet it says that Israel allowed only two hundred per day to cross through the alternative crossing point, implying that this was a tiny amount—when it was actually twice what was needed. The eager reporter did not even do this trivial arithmetic in his rush to incriminate the Israelis.

Seventh, the Palestinians are cited as refusing to allow the alternative crossing because it violates some agreements. It's hard to know whether to cry or laugh at such a complaint. After conducting almost four years of terror, they're bothered by the violation of an agreement? Did those agreements allow for bombing the border crossings?

Then there is the statement that the United States raised the issue, implying that the Americans had criticized the stance—which never happened. There is also a reference to Egypt recommending Israeli aid, but not a hint of what Egypt did to help people on its soil. The Palestinians were stranded in Egypt, not in Argentina, entirely because of the acts of their terrorist countrymen and of their stubborn officials who rejected the alternative crossing.

Finally, there is the story of the dead bodies. One wonders if the authorities of the United States, where the *New York Times* is published, would have allowed the bodies of two people who died from unknown ailments in an Egyptian hospital in Cairo to enter the United States without any serious medical scrutiny.

All of the above distortions are contained in one little misleading news item. Is it all accidental? Is it deliberate? Is it just sloppy journalism? If the distortions were inadvertent, how many sloppy stories have appeared that twist the truth in the opposite direction? If they were deliberate, what is the motivation?

On its own, the entire story is unimportant. I assume that relatively few people read it, and fewer still remember it today. But such things nevertheless create an impression—in this case, of heartless, cruel Israelis preventing ailing well-meaning Palestinians from coming home. The Palestinians have names, diarrhea, and miscarriages. The Israelis are busy preventing families from reclaiming the bodies of their deceased relatives. The entire story is told as if it happened on the Swiss-Italian border. No terror, no danger, no suicides.

Five months after this story was published, a huge quantity of explosives, brought in through an underground tunnel, blew up the same crossing point, killing many of the Israeli guards. The digging of the tunnel started just before the date of the *New York Times* story. The Israelis received a tip about a planned attack, closed the crossing point, tried to discover the plot, failed, and paid the price months later.

This story is not an extraordinary case. It is no more than standard practice. If my analysis sounds petty and tiresome, the conclusion is clear and undeniable.

Such things go on day after day, year after year. And together they create a fertile ground for hatred toward Israel, for calls for boycotts and sanctions, for accusations and defamation. The report from Gaza is carefully crafted to avoid explicit lies; the writer could never be sued for malicious intent. When you review it after learning the real story, think back to our fictitious September 11 news item. This is the respectable free press of the free world—and hardly the worst example drawn from its ranks, just an average one.

"All the news that's fit to print."

—21—

SOME REFUGEES ARE MORE EQUAL THAN OTHERS

Most Palestinian refugees were displaced fifty-seven years ago by less than the distance between New York and Philadelphia or Zurich and Basel. Their great-grandchildren are still in refugee camps, only because someone is still hoping to send them to destroy Israel.

In the past sixty-five years, tens of millions of refugees have found themselves removed from their homes by acts of war. The refugees were Polish, Vietnamese, Sudanese, German, Kurd, Bangladeshi, Czech, Chinese, Israeli, Pakistani, Bosnian, Palestinian, Burundi, Korean, and countless other nationalities. Of all the millions of people who became refugees in the 1940s and 1950s, the only ones who still count themselves as refugees, who have never been settled in their new places, and who live at the expense of the nations of the world are the Palestinians. Every single refugee, everywhere, is a personal tragedy. But if a self-perpetuated tragedy is deliberately extended over fifty-seven years, it is an entirely different story, especially when the refugee status is imposed on the children, the grandchildren, and the great-grandchildren of many of the original refugees, long after the first generation passed away.

In fact, the United Nations has essentially classified all the refugees in the world into three groups: the Palestinians, the Jews, and "all the rest." The rules for the three groups are clear and almost self-evident. "All the rest" are dealt with by the United Nations High Commissioner on Refugees (UNHCR), who is responsible for a variety of emergency humanitarian programs for helping refugees almost everywhere but in the Holy Land.

The Palestinian refugees are a special, privileged class. There is a special, separate UN agency, the United Nations Relief and Work Agency (UNRWA), whose principal duty is to perpetuate their status as refugees; to prevent any attempt to settle them; and to provide them, their children, their grandchildren, and the next generations with so-called humanitarian assistance. Its budget per capita is much higher than the budget for normal, second-class refugees. Not one other refugee in the world is deliberately encouraged to remain a refugee. Fifty-seven years later, UNRWA also employs, according to its own head, members of Hamas and other similar organizations. This international peacekeeping body, then, is directly financing terror under a "humanitarian" cover.

The third category is the Jews. Millions of Jews became refugees at roughly the same time as the Palestinians. Many had lost everything in Europe as a result of the Holocaust. Numerous others had to leave their houses and property in the Arab countries, from Iraq to Morocco, and flee—many to Israel, others to various other countries. None of these Jewish refugees were helped by the United Nations. All were settled long ago in their new environments.

Many of the refugees, in almost all countries and all cases, were displaced by considerable distances—sometimes hundreds of kilometers, sometimes more. Many of them had to adjust to a new culture and a new language. Most of the Palestinian refugees were displaced by distances comparable with those within the size of a large city. All of them live in an area where the culture, religion, and language are their own. The infamous Jenin Palestinian refugee camp, which became a major center of terror and murder in the past few years, has been in existence for fifty-seven years. Most of its inhabitants were born there, including all the terrorists, but the small number who actually came from elsewhere came from places closer to Jenin than Heathrow Airport is to the city of London or Kennedy airport to Manhattan. Most dwellers in the Gaza Strip refugee camps were born there during the past fifty-seven years. But the older ones, who were indeed true refugees fifty-seven years ago, came from places that could be reached within half an hour by car, perhaps an hour in heavy traffic.

The cost of building a $50,000 apartment for every so-called Palestinian refugee household during the past twenty-five years would have been less than 1 percent of the oil income of the Arab states alone. These families are mostly headed by people who never lived elsewhere; they are "genetic refugees" in the sense that they have inherited the refugee label from their parents or grandparents. But the rich Arab oil countries have never lifted a finger for these Palestinian genetic refugees, except for some support for religious institutions and terror organizations. When Israel conquered Gaza and the West Bank in 1967, specific plans to settle the refugees in their places permanently were worked out. With the active support of the UN agency UNRWA, which had a clear interest of perpetuating itself, the Palestinians objected vehemently and blocked the plans. They would accept only the settling of the refugees instead of Israel.

There are dozens of books and heated debates on the question of how the Palestinian refugees became refugees. No other group of refugees from the 1940s or 1950s has had such attention. When you start a war and lose it, the results are always grim. It is absolutely clear that some of the refugees escaped from their homes out of fear of the war, some were driven from their homes by the advancing Israeli army, and many left after their own leadership issued calls to abandon their homes so they could return victoriously a few weeks later. Alas, their leadership misled them; they were never able to return. It is also clear that, in every one of the dozen or so cases where the Arabs succeeded in conquering Jewish villages in the war of 1948, not one Jew was allowed to stay in his or her house. Many were murdered, and all the others were expelled.

It is my humble opinion that, six decades later, the various circumstances that caused Palestinians to become refugees are not very relevant. War is cruel. The war was started by the Palestinians, who did not accept the partition of Palestine. They were joined by the armies of all the neighboring Arab states. They were defeated. Had they won, not one Jew would have remained alive. Is there another case in history in which the side that initiated the war and was defeated has demanded that the outcome be reversed and that they receive compensation just so they could start a new war from the same positions?

It is absolutely clear that most of the so-called Palestinian refugees are in no sense true refugees. They were born, raised, married, and have had children and even grandchildren in the places where they live now. Some have never set foot in the place from which they were supposedly refugees. If you count them as refugees, many third-generation Americans, including John Kerry, are refugees. It is equally clear that those who are true refugees continue to have this status because they want it, because they serve as pawns in the desire of others to destroy Israel, or because the United Nations has an elaborate bureaucracy whose only purpose is to perpetuate their status. In the meantime, a similar number of Jewish refugees from all the Arab countries, some of whom were originally poor and others who left all their considerable property to the Arabs, have been absorbed by Israel while it was still much poorer than the Arab countries, with the help of Jews elsewhere in the world and with no help from the United Nations.

Refugee camps photograph very well when an army enters to search for suicide murderers or missile launchers. Nothing perpetuates the fallacy of the Palestinian underdog as well as the phony legends about the refugees. They are held by their own people in deliberate misery, for generations, in order to maintain the propaganda edge. They are misled to believe that one day they will inherit the houses built by the Israelis in Israel. Many of them, with the encouragement of the Palestinian leadership, proudly display keys, real or fake, for their deserted homes, to which they will one day return—and which almost never exist. It is a tragic and cynical manipulation of these poor people by a leadership whose only goal is the total destruction of another nation.

The slogan of the refugees is "the right of return." This is the Palestinian translation of the phrase "eliminating the Jews." "The right of return" sounds noble and innocent; European ears find it appealing. Somehow the Sudete Germans, the Pakistani Muslims, and the black Sudanese Africans apparently do not qualify for this privilege, even though they have no plans to eliminate any nation. When the Palestinians talk about a "just and lasting peace," that is often a code for "the right of return," which in turn, means "eliminating the Jews." It is very important to be familiar with this Middle Eastern dictionary. Most of the world is not.

I write these words with great pain and regret. Like many other left-of-center Israelis, I believed that the Oslo agreements of 1993 had put an end to the ambition to eliminate Israel. We supported them. We ignored those who warned us that Arafat had not changed—that the elimination of all the Jews from Israel remained his goal. Events in the region proved us wrong. Arafat went to his death without ever changing. "The right of return" is still the leading Palestinian slogan, the group's one serious demand. It is not surprising that almost all the strongest left-wing Israeli critics of the Sharon government would never entertain the possibility of a "right of return." They support a Palestinian state in addition to Israel, but not in its place. They want peace and reconciliation, but not an elimination of the Jews. As long as the so-called refugees and their great-grandchildren are maintained as such, deliberately and with UN support, and as long as the phrase "right of return" is still mentioned outside the history books, there can be no solution. However, once this obstacle is eliminated—once the Palestinians fully realize that Israel is here to stay and accept the permanent settlement of the refugees in their current places—peace will be within reach.

—22—

REWRITING HISTORY

If I told you that the towers of the World Trade Center never ex-isted, that Julius Caesar was British, and that the American Civil War did not happen, would you ever pay attention to any-thing else I told you?

History books and national memories are never impartial. There is no Trafalgar Square in Paris, nothing is named after Salah-ad-Din in the Vatican, and Garibaldi is no hero to the Austrians. But the French admit that Napoleon was defeated in Russia, the British version of the birth of the United States is not much different from the American one, and the Germans should be commended for teaching so much about the Holocaust in their schools.

Jesus Christ was born in Bethlehem in Judea. Yes, J-u-d-e-a, which is Yehuda (the biblical son of Jacob) in the original Hebrew. The many European versions of this word include *Judaic, Jude, Yehudi, Judah,* and *Jew.* The name *Bethlehem* means "house of bread" in biblical Hebrew and in the modern Hebrew spoken today in Jerusalem supermarkets. There is a theory that the name Bethlehem originally came from an ancient pagan God named Lachmu, worshipped before the Jews arrived there more than three thousand years ago, but by the time of the Old Testament it already had its Hebrew name.

But the Palestinian leadership, especially the late Arafat, has claimed that Jesus was Palestinian. Was he an Arab? No. Muslim? Of course not. Philistine? Of course not. We are sorry, but Jesus was Jewish. Should this fact be relevant to today's problems in the Middle East? Probably not. Again, however, when people feel free to lie so blatantly, it's wise to think twice before accepting any of their other statements.

Why are they lying? In this case, because they want to create an analogy between the suffering of Jesus—a symbol of peace and love—and the fate of terrorists and murderers. At the same time, the analogy appeals to those anti-Semites who still blame the Jews for killing Jesus. A perfect ploy!

The Jewish temple, history tells us, was built and destroyed in Jerusalem—but not according to numerous Arab sources, including Arafat and his friends. This is a Jewish fabrication, they insist. After all, having fabricated the Holocaust, couldn't the Jews have invented the legend of the temple as well? Perhaps the fact that the sun rises in the east is also a Jewish fabrication? Certainly, in their minds, September 11 was an obvious Jewish plot.

Hearing such lies, it's difficult not to ask yourself: "Why make a fuss about this? This is a lunatic fringe. No serious person would believe it." The problem is that these are more than just the remarks of fringe groups: They're official positions codified by government organs in Saudi Arabia, Egypt, and most other Arab countries. They are repeated by religious leaders and by the inevitable Palestinian leadership.

If you were an American journalist or a European head of state and you paid a moment's attention to these systematic and consistent lies, why would you ever listen to, or quote, the word of such people? Yet every day their latest proclamations are reported as gospel, without any reminder that these people have also propounded such absurd allegations.

Palestine is the name given to the area by the ancient Greeks, after the Philistines who once populated the land. The Philistines were a non-Semitic people who came from somewhere in the Aegean Sea, probably the Greek islands. By the time the word *Palestine* began to be used, the Philistines were long extinct. The most famous Philistine was Goliath, the giant who was defeated by little David, later king of Israel. In those days, they had it right about the underdog.

Obviously, there isn't the remotest connection between the ancient Philistines, with their origin, religion, culture, and language, and anything Arab or Muslim. The first Arabs came to the area many centuries after the Greeks coined the name Palestine, long after the Philistines disappeared, and longer after the Jews had arrived. Islam would not enter the picture for centuries.

The Philistines, then, lived approximately three thousand years ago in what is today the Gaza Strip and small parts of southern Israel and disappeared from history a thousand years before the first Arab or the first Muslim set foot in the Holy Land. The name Palestine was the invention of the Greek rulers; the names *Israel* and *Judea* go back approximately three millennia.

You may say that none of this matters. You may claim that the circumstances of two thousand or even two hundred years ago, when my family arrived, should not influence today's events. This is a perfectly reasonable point of view, as is the opposite view, which argues that history is relevant. But to create an absolutely fallacious history is quite a different exercise. It is a part of the elaborate network of nonstop lies that has permanently and consistently accompanied the Arab-Israeli conflict.

We have already mentioned that the political entity referred to as Palestine by the Palestinians existed as such for only twenty-seven years, from 1921 to 1948. At all other times in history, the political divisions in the area were different—and for centuries there was no clear distinction between the inhabitants of the areas now occupied by Syria, Lebanon, Jordan, Israel, and the Palestinians. Hundreds of millions of Europeans and Americans have been continuously fed the wrong impression that a place called Palestine, populated by the Palestinian people, was for centuries the home of this nation until they were expelled in 1948 by the invading Jews.

When California still belonged to Mexico, more than a century before 1948, the Jews were already the majority in Jerusalem. Most Europeans and Americans have no idea that this is true. Nor do they have any idea that the "country" of Palestine last existed as an independent state when the ancient Israelites ruled it two thousand years ago.

Today, unbelievably enough, there is debate over whether the country was empty or densely populated when the significant Jewish immigration started at the end of the nineteenth century (the period when my two grandmothers grew up there). This is the issue on which the Palestinians base the fallacy that the flourishing region was "stolen by the Jews."

Listen to the two sides of the debate and judge for yourself. Some zealous Israelis claim that the country was almost empty. They love to quote the report of Mark Twain, who visited the Holy Land in the nineteenth century and wrote that it was very sparsely populated. The Palestinians vehemently deny the idea, pointing to other sources—not necessarily more reliable—who claim that the entire population may have reached five hundred thousand by the end of the nineteenth century. Let us assume that this claim is so—that, for a change, the Palestinian propagandists are telling the truth.

A population of half a million in the full area of what was then Palestine—which included today's Jordan—would mean an average of roughly four people per square kilometer (or ten per square mile). Even if we assume that these five hundred thousand people all lived west of the Jordan River, which is hardly certain, it would mean an average population density of eighteen people per square kilometer in that area, excluding the entire area of today's Kingdom of Jordan. So, even by the Palestinians' own contentions, the population density was somewhere between four and eighteen people per square kilometer. Does this constitute "densely populated" or almost empty?

Population density numbers are very confusing. Most of us have no strong feeling for what ten people per square kilometer—or thirty, one hundred, or three hundred—might look like.

Let us make some comparisons. The population densities of Israel, India, Belgium, Lebanon, and Japan all exceed three hundred per square kilometer. Egypt, which is largely a desert, has seventy people per square kilometer. The American states of Nevada, Colorado, and Utah, which are very sparsely populated, have between eight and eighteen people per square kilometer; so does Finland, an almost empty country. By the Palestinians' own numbers, then, the area was no more densely settled than some of the least populous states of the American West are today.

But let us do something much more interesting. Please close your eyes and imagine that you are having a very peculiar dream. You are visiting the island of Manhattan. In your dream, it is populated by the same density of people that the Palestinians claim to have existed in the Holy Land when the significant Jewish immigration started before the year 1900. You believe the Palestinian claims that half a million people lived west of the Jordan and that the country was densely populated. How many people do you think you will find, in this hypothetical dream, living in Manhattan? Care to guess?

Open your eyes. The answer is one thousand.

I know—you don't believe your eyes. So I'll write it again: one thousand people. If you still can't believe it, do the math yourself. If the entire population of the island of Manhattan were one thousand people, it would be as dense as Israel or the Palestinian district of the Ottoman Empire was in 1900, according to the Palestinians.

Does that feel empty? Full? Decide for yourself. If Manhattan with a total of one thousand inhabitants is considered full, Palestine was full of Palestinians.

An equally eye-opening observation is this: The Palestinians always complain—rightfully, I believe—about the few unnecessary Jewish settlements in the Gaza Strip, where eight thousand Jews live among more than a million Palestinians. These are the small settlements that are slated for evacuation under the Sharon disengagement plan. Imagine, God forbid, that all the Palestinians in Gaza should disappear, abandoning all their towns and villages and leaving the entire

Gaza Strip in the hands of this tiny number of Jewish settlers. If no one else moved in, the remaining population density of the Gaza Strip (eight thousand people taking the place of more than a million!) would still be higher than that of nineteenth-century Palestine, even according to the Palestinian claims.

Need we say more? Regardless of whether Mark Twain's word can be taken at face value, it is clear that this piece of land, consisting of mostly bare hills and of swamps in the valleys, was very sparsely inhabited. It had a nonexistent economy, no industry, very little agriculture, and not one town that boasted anything close to fifty thousand people.

Won't some people insist that nineteenth-century figures are irrelevant—that we should concentrate on today's situation? Yes—but we can't have it both ways. We must either forget about history and focus on contemporary issues, or tell the truth about history. We do not have the option of invoking a fictitious history when it suits our current needs. This is exactly what the Arab world has been doing for years in marketing its story to the Western world, with an amazing degree of success. The Israelis, who have been successful in so many other areas, have failed miserably when it comes to disseminating the simple facts.

I have personal reasons for calling attention to these historical questions. It was during the 1890s that my two grandfathers arrived by (different) boats to Jaffa as teenagers. How large was this "harbor," the only one in the country at that time? We can answer this question even today, for it has grown only marginally since then. It is a typical small village harbor, the kind you can find in hundreds of villages all around the Mediterranean. The main harbors of Israel are now elsewhere; the Jaffa harbor has remained more or less as it was. Take one look at this harbor, and you'll have a sense of how populated the country was.

When my two grandfathers arrived, one of my grandmothers had already been in the Holy Land for a decade; the other side had lived there for three generations. My grandfather Aba (meaning "father" in Hebrew) built a small factory of water pumps, producing the first pumps for the entire tiny Arab and Jewish farming population. My great-grandfather Zerach (same name as the biblical son of Judah, son of Jacob) was one of the first watchmakers in the country. He installed the first clock on the famous clock tower in Jaffa one hundred years ago. These were some of the people whose existence has been denied by the Palestinians.

LIFE NEAR THE END ZONE

Two attempts at serve are allowed in tennis, three tries in the high jump, and four downs in American football. Why are the Arabs allowed an unlimited number of attempts to eliminate Israel and its Jews?

The ball is on the one-yard line. It is tenth down and goal to go. This is the Super Bowl of the Middle East, between the Jihad Martyrs, who seem to have clinched first place in the Arab League, and the Jerusalem Chaos, the flag bearer of the Jewish teams. The playing field is one hundred yards long, as always in American football, but the action surrounds the one-yard line of Jerusalem. The Jihad has the ball.

"Just a moment," you say. "What do you mean, *tenth down?* There are only four downs in American football." In this particular game, the rules are different. Whenever Jerusalem sacks the Jihad quarterback or intercepts the ball, the referee stops the game and team Jihad gets to start again from the one-yard line. For the Jihad, the number of potential downs is unlimited. And there is one more rule: If the Jihad scores even once, the Jerusalem team is executed. Under these rules, the term *end zone* is given a whole new meaning.

The Jerusalem Chaos always has its back to the goal line, one yard from total defeat. It manages again and again to stop the attacks and sometimes even to advance. But the referee always sends the Jerusalem team backward, claiming one technical violation or another. The Jihad team has many more players on the field, more substitutes, and much more money. It is always one yard away from the goal line, trying everything to score a touchdown. Yet most of the international crowd cheers for them—as the underdog. Yes, that's right: *the underdog.*

The total land area of the five Arab countries adjacent to Israel is at least one hundred times larger than Israel. These are the countries that attack Israel again and again. The Israeli border is always one yard from the proverbial goal line, but the potential for Israel's physical annihilation is not proverbial at all. Nevertheless, the chorus chants nonstop, "The Arabs are the poor underdog. They are refugees. They are desperate." And the crowd buys it.

There was an old Jewish story, from the time of the Russian pogroms, about the four "heroic" Jews who went for a walk in the forest and saw a single bulky Gentile coming. There was no one else in sight. Said one of the Jews, "Let's run away. We are alone here." When the Arab world, with its huge population, large land area, and abundant natural resources, looks at a map of the region, doesn't it notice that the name *Israel* must be written on the sea because there isn't enough room to write it inside the territory? "Look at Israel," they say, "We are the underdog."

The first Arab wave of terror against the Jewish community—the "first down"—took place as early as 1921. The next wave came in 1929, when my great-uncle Moshe Harari and a group of other Jews were murdered in the streets of Jaffa by an Arab mob. The climax of this "second down" was a massacre of the entire Jewish community of Hebron. The "third down" was the Arab terror against the British and the Jews from 1936 to 1939; then came World War II, in which the Palestinians strongly supported Hitler, and then the 1948 war, in which Egypt, Jordan, Lebanon, Syria, and Iraq, as well as the Palestinians, rejected the UN resolution that established a Jewish state and an Arab Palestinian state and attacked the fledgling Jewish state. The

Egyptian air force bombed Tel Aviv one day after the new state was declared; they destroyed an apartment house near our home and scored a direct hit at the central bus station, killing numerous civilians and blowing up the only double-decker bus in Tel Aviv—thus terminating my childhood dream to be the driver of such a bus.

All around the world, from the 1940s on, borders have changed as the result of warfare. The maps of Europe, Asia, and Africa have been completely redrawn. Almost all new borders were recognized by all nations. Historic India was dissected into India and Pakistan; later, Bangladesh split from Pakistan. Poland was "moved" to the west at the expense of Germany and to Russia's benefit. Russia annexed the Baltic countries and pieces of Finland, Rumania, Hungary, and Czechoslovakia; the last-named eventually split into two. In the end, the Soviet Union itself broke apart. Yugoslavia became five or six different countries. Indochina became Vietnam, Laos, and Cambodia. Korea and Vietnam were divided; Vietnam, finally, was reunited. From Eritrea to Mongolia, from Namibia to Yemen, the story goes on.

There is only one war whose outcome has never been recognized: The defeat of the five Arab states and the Palestinians by Israel. Jordan used the opportunity to annex the West Bank, against all international resolutions. Only Pakistan and the United Kingdom recognized this annexation. But the matter was never brought to the UN. Jordan was never condemned; no nation showed any desire to sanction or boycott it, even though it controlled a piece of land that was clearly outside its territory, expelled the small number of Jews who lived in it for decades, and refused to allow any Jew to pray in their holiest site, the Western Wall of the Temple in Jerusalem. Egypt has done the same with the Gaza Strip, the only part of the former Palestine that the invading Egyptian army still controlled after its defeat. These two occupations, it was said, were "in tune with the international mood." And it should be noted that neither occupying nation offered its occupied Palestinians an independent state, although they had nineteen years to do so. The occupied Palestinians were not allowed to complain very much by their Arab brothers.

At the same time, Israel's borders were only half recognized. Even the country's greatest friends refused to recognize Israel's capital, Jerusalem, even though the true capital included only the western part of Jerusalem, excluding the holiest Jewish places. The excuse of objecting to an "Israeli occupation" did not yet exist. But the world community considered the Jews unworthy of having even West Jerusalem as its capital city and established all embassies in Tel Aviv.

For nineteen years, from 1948 to 1967, there were numerous Palestinian terror attacks on Israel. When I was fifteen years old, working with my high school class in a Kibbutz called Nirim near the Gaza Strip, we came under intensive Egyptian artillery fire from Gaza aimed at this civilian village. Almost fifty years later, Palestinians from Gaza are still shelling Israeli villages and towns. On the way back to Tel Aviv in spring 1956, we passed a number of casualties resulting from an attack on a civilian vehicle perpetrated by Palestinian terrorists inside Israel, quite far from the border. Almost fifty years later, Palestinians are still blowing up civilian buses within Israel. All of this was happening in the 1950s with no Israeli occupation, while the West Bank was Jordanian and Gaza was Egyptian. Yet today's terror is still characterized as a "response to the Israeli occupation." And what about the terror campaigns of the 1950s? Well, those have been forgotten—erased from the Arab history books.

Again, we should remember: There are two sides to this dispute. The Jewish state has not always been right, nor has it always considered the rights and the feelings of its neighbors. There is room for criticism on all sides. But I know of no case in which such history has been so thoroughly rewritten by a group of nations, their political and religious leaders, their masses, and the international media as has occurred in the Middle East.

One day, historians will devote serious study to a very interesting question: How did the Palestinians succeed in fooling so many people for such a long time, without the entire world standing up and saying: "For God's sake, if you wish to get anywhere, please stop these lies"?

Rewriting history is only one aspect of this saga. We must learn from the past, but the present is always much more important. Regardless of how important history may be to current events, no one would dispute the importance of understanding the circumstances of the present.

Consider, for example, Jerusalem.

For centuries, the city of Jerusalem was under Muslim rule, controlled by the Muslim Ottomans, Egyptians, and Jordanians, among others. They never made it their capital city. Suddenly, in 1967, when all of Jerusalem came under Israeli rule for the first time since the days of Jesus, the Palestinians remembered that they needed to have Jerusalem as their capital. Although it had never been a Muslim capital and had always been the capital city of the Jews, it was decided that Jerusalem must now be the Palestinian capital "for obvious historic reasons." Images of Arafat in his office always showed a huge photo of Jerusalem on the wall behind him. That photo was not there before 1967. The capital of Jordan has always been Amman, never Jerusalem.

Like spoiled children, the Palestinians want a toy just because it belongs to another boy.

When Jordan held the Old City of Jerusalem, Jews were prevented from visiting their holiest shrines, and no one else protested or cared. In 1967, when Israel gained control of the entire city, the world suddenly remembered that freedom of religion in Jerusalem and free access to their holy places for people of all religions were important. Well, better late than never—yet wasn't their timing a telling coincidence?

For more than one hundred and fifty years, Jerusalem has had a Jewish majority. But Palestinian logic has its own rules. Why must Jerusalem be the Palestinians' capital city? Well, because it is a holy city for the Muslims. The proverbial taxi driver in me has a simple question: If the Muslims need their holy cities to be their capitals, why isn't Mecca the capital of Saudi Arabia? Or, for that matter, why not Islam's second holiest city, Medina? Why isn't Najaf, the holiest place for the Shiite Muslims, the capital of predominantly Shiite Iraq?

You needn't try to answer these questions. They have no answers. There is no reason that a city with a long-standing Jewish majority and

Muslim minority, which is a holy place for the Jews, Christians, and Muslims—in that order—should be claimed by the Palestinians as their capital. But it's difficult to stop people from trying to fool the world—and those who prove talented at such things may even succeed.

The current wave of terror, as we've seen, is billed "an uprising against Israeli occupation." How convincing! But the Palestine Liberation Organization (PLO) was established—and its name coined—before 1967, when the West Bank was Jordanian and the Gaza Strip was Egyptian. Where exactly was the Palestine that needed to be liberated by this organization before 1967? Well, no one remembers to ask this question. But the purpose has always been, and still is, to liberate all of Israel from the disturbing presence of the Jews. The terrorist attacks before 1967 have been forgotten. Who wants to look back? And if tomorrow a Palestinian state should exist next to Israel, will these attacks against Israel continue? Most Palestinian organizations respond honestly in the affirmative. True, there are some Palestinians—although not many—who are willing to consider a two-state solution, a peaceful coexistence with Israel. But the question remains: Would this be a permanent existence or a temporary arrangement until the next war arises?

Can Israel make a deal with the rest of Globania? We will have a Palestinian state next to Israel, but if it ever again sends terrorists into Israel or launches any type of artillery, the entire world will be morally obliged to exclude it entirely from the family of nations and to encourage Israel to defend itself.

I realize that I must be incredibly naive to suggest this, and to believe that the world would honor such a pledge. Yet exactly such an agreement was tried after the 1956 Sinai War, when Israel returned all of Sinai and Gaza to Egypt with clear UN guarantees against any further Egyptian attacks. It took the UN exactly twenty-four hours to disappear in May 1967, when Egypt blockaded Israel and moved its entire huge army to the Israeli border.

Most of the world, led by the Arab countries, recommends a return to the 1967 borders. And what is so sacred about these borders? Does anyone remember how these borders were created? They are accidental lines, marking the positions of the opposing armies on the day of the ceasefire at the end of the 1948 war. This so-called Green Line passes through the middle of several Arab villages, separating family members from one another. It passes through the middle of Jerusalem, splitting the city. Until 1967, no Arab country was happy with this border. The Palestinians never accepted it. Suddenly, this accidental line, which has been valid for only nineteen years and has existed only on paper for exactly twice as long—thirty-eight years—has become the dream boundary of the Arab world and all of its supporters.

Because there are more than a million Arabs on the Israeli side of the Green Line and a couple hundred thousand Jews on the other side, shouldn't the final border be determined by direct, open-minded negotiations with give and take? Perhaps it should be guided by an attempt to minimize the minorities on both sides to avoid friction in the future? Today there are Israeli settlements in the midst of densely populated Palestinian areas; these should have never been built and cannot stay. There are others near the old border, similar to many large Arab villages on the other side of the old border. Wouldn't it make sense to try some trading of land, moving the border both ways, rather than moving people and destroying their houses and their schools? "Unacceptable," say the Arabs. "All Arabs in Israel must stay. All Jews in the West Bank must leave."

This demand is quite puzzling. Here are Palestinian Arabs, who live in Israel as Israeli citizens. According to the Palestinian Authority, they are suffering in Israel from "an apartheid regime run by the racist Jews," while independent Palestine will be "an exemplary democracy." When some people suggest that Israeli Arabs who live near the border should stay where they are (with their homes and lands) while the border is moved (at Israel's expense) to include these Arabs in the "Palestinian democracy" rather than in the "Israeli apartheid," they flatly refuse. "This is a racist proposal," they claim.

How interesting!

—24—

FOOLING MOST OF THE PEOPLE, MOST OF THE TIME

You can fool most of the people all the time. You can fool all the people most of the time. But you cannot fool all the people all the time, unless you are the Palestinians.

Two unemployed friends were discussing their search for work.

"They asked me how old I was," said one. "I hesitated. If I added a few years to my real age, they might have refused to hire someone so old. If I said I was younger than I really was, they might think I was inexperienced."

"So why didn't you tell them the truth?" asked his friend.

"Well, I didn't think of it."

It is absolutely clear that, if the Palestinians had ever chosen to tell the truth, their situation would have been much better. They could have already established their own state and might have seen their economy take off. Alas, the idea never caught on with them, and the result is a national tragedy. They're so busy fooling the rest of the world that they often forget they invented these lies—and start believing in them.

This applies to ancient history, to the history of a century ago, to the events of the past fifty years, to the story of the refugees, to their terror campaign, to the struggle for Jerusalem, and to just about everything else related to the Palestinians' tragic, self-afflicted, desperate condition.

Their success in fooling the world is largely based on the fact that enlightened people simply cannot believe that a people could lie so systematically and consistently. It also draws strength from anti-Semitic undercurrents in contemporary society, from the natural human inclination to sympathize with the losers in any battle, and from persistent illusions about the exotic Middle East. Some current episodes tell part of the story. There are many others.

The wall or fence or barrier (choose your favorite term) that Israel built to protect itself against suicide murderers, which has proven extremely effective, runs near the Green Line in some areas and away from it in others. In certain places, it cuts brutally through Palestinian fields or inhabited areas, and in such places the Israeli Supreme Court has ordered a change of location. But the fence has already saved many innocent lives and thwarted numerous murders. For the Palestinians, this is reason enough to condemn it, to claim that "it creates a ghetto," and to talk international organizations into demanding that it be dismantled.

A ghetto? Israel is surrounded by hundreds of millions of Arabs on all sides, many of them eager to destroy it—the Palestinians regularly send murderers to wedding halls and shopping malls—and Israel is creating a ghetto? But when Israel listens to them and moves the fence to accommodate Palestinian demands, here is a typical example of what happens:

The Arab village of Baka in the north of Israel was essentially split in two fifty-seven years ago. The war of 1948 and the Green Line separated West Baka, which ended up in Israel, from East Baka in Jordan. The border passed between houses and separated members of the same family, who were unable to see each other for nineteen years. Since 1967, the two parts of Baka have been reunited and once again have become intimately connected. Since that time, new Arab houses have been built on the old Green Line between the two parts, illegally, but no one has touched them. When the famous new wall was constructed, it was built east of the Green Line in order to preserve the new houses and avoid severing the population once again. "An outrage!" screamed the Palestinians. "This is a land grab." Israel destroyed the fence already standing there, along with the illegal Arab houses on the old Green Line, and moved the fence to the Green Line, once again separating East and West Baka to satisfy the demands of those who could not care less about their brothers.

Not far from Baka is the refugee camp of Jenin, most of whose residents, including all terrorists, were born long after 1948 and could not possibly define themselves as refugees. The camp has become one of the main centers of terror; some of the worst murderers were recruited, trained, and dispatched from there. Following the 2001 suicide murder of twenty-seven elderly people in the Passover Seder in an Israeli hotel, Israel embarked on a military operation to disable the terrorists there.

It would have taken a couple of hours to level the Jenin camp from the air, which would have eliminated most of the terrorists without any Israeli casualties. Yet Israel never even considered doing so because it would also have involved killing hundreds or thousands of innocent people. Instead the Israeli army went into the labyrinth of narrow alleys in the camp, entering houses that were booby-trapped, facing fire from each window and street corner, and encountering countless mines and explosive devices in their search for the murderers. The action cost the army dearly in human life: More than twenty Israeli soldiers were killed because the army chose to avoid hurting innocent civilians. It is difficult to think of another army in the world that would have risked and lost so many lives at a time of war just to avoid enemy civilian casualties. The total number of Palestinians killed in the operation, which lasted several days, was approximately fifty. Most were active terrorists and murderers; only a few were bystanders. On the third day of the operation, nevertheless, the Palestinian fabrication industry started: "A massacre." "Genocide." "More than five hundred Palestinians murdered."

"Israel is hiding the bodies." This went on and on for weeks, led by the most senior Palestinian leaders.

There was not one major news organization in the world that refused to repeat the lies. The United Nations immediately jumped on the bandwagon, bypassing any need for hard facts in its rush to condemn, reproach, and accuse. At first, due to Israel's total incompetence in matters of press relations, the press was not allowed to enter the camp to see for itself. Even so, when faced with two versions of the events, the press chose to trumpet the lies. Later, when the truth finally came out, almost no one apologized. On the contrary, new lies were produced to justify the previous ones. A photo of an Israeli tank was combined with a different photo of Palestinian prisoners lying on the ground, so that it appeared that the tank was driving over them. This photo was a total fake, of course, but it was a good enough fake that many newspapers published it, claiming later that "it was clear that these were two photos printed one above the other." If it was so clear, why didn't anyone print the photo of the prisoners on top and the tank below or perhaps side by side? Simply because lies sell better than the truth.

Perhaps one day the full story of Jenin will be told: how people who were displaced fifty-seven years ago (typically by no more than a twenty-minute drive), as a result of a war they started, deliberately remained penniless refugees instead of settling permanently in their new home; how their grandchildren were trained and financed as murderers to try to destroy another nation; how they burst into a wedding party in a blaze of gunfire, killed old people, exploded buses, attacked civilians in the streets, and booby-trapped their entire camp, waiting for the counterattack; how, against the normal behavior of any other country, the Israeli army risked and lost the lives of more than twenty officers and soldiers just to minimize casualties among Palestinian civilians; and how what followed was an unbelievable and unforgivable campaign of lies and defamation.

There are many such stories. The well-oiled machine churns along, and the world press never stops for a moment to say: "These people lie so often, perhaps we should check their claims more carefully."

Another astonishingly successful public relations campaign mounted by the terrorists is the "body count" argument. Many more Germans than Americans died in World War II. Does that make Hitler right? Does that make him the poor underdog, deserving someone's sympathy? Does that make the United States the aggressor? Of course not. If three suicide murderers detonate a bomb in a busy shopping mall and kill "only" two innocent people, does that 3 : 2 ratio prove that the murderers are the ones being attacked?

When Hamas sends rockets into the heart of Israeli villages and towns, hitting apartment houses and kindergartens, killing children, they call it "a war of liberation." When the Israeli army succeeds in striking back at the rocket launchers, the Palestinians start firing at them from the busy center of their own towns, using innocent civilians and their houses as shields. When Israeli technology succeeds in accurately hitting them even then, with relatively small damage to others, they bring children to surround the rocket launchers. Finally, they pull the ultimate trump card: As a result of all of these dastardly strategies, the number of Palestinian casualties eventually exceeds Israelis—and Israel is deemed the aggressor.

The logic is impeccable: Because you're losing the war—a dirty war that you have initiated—you must have the support of the world. Hitler must be kicking himself in hell, wondering, "How did I miss this trick?" Amazingly, most respected Western newspapers repeat this absurd argument without comment; the United Nations publishes a report announcing how many people have been killed on each side, implying that the side with more casualties is necessarily the victim—and including even the suicide murderers themselves in the count.

Before long, the speaker of the Greek parliament was accusing Israel of genocide. (Was Israel any more guilty of genocide than the Greeks who defended their country against German attacks in World War II?) In Norway, some politicians revived the claim that Israel is an apartheid state—a charge that revealed their ignorance about both Israel and apartheid itself. A Portuguese Nobel Laureate visited Ramallah, listened to a few hours of blatant lies, and announced that Israel was behaving like the Nazis. Syria's President Assad, head of a regime that murdered tens of thousands of its own citizens and hosts some of the worst terror organizations in the world, accused Israel of war crimes; thereafter he was elected to the UN Security Council, with the support of most Western countries. All of these remarks were repeated again and again (with proper reference and "without taking sides") by the media, and the disinformation juggernaut rolled on.

Some of the people who repeat such lies are fools, some are naive, and some are anti-Semitic. Some, no doubt, are all of the above. But the industry of hatred is fed by the industry of lies, and both work overtime to produce unprecedented volume. This vast machine is aimed at delegitimizing the state of Israel, dehumanizing the Jews everywhere, and preparing the ground for yet another attempt at a "final solution to the Jewish problem." The burning synagogues in France and Belgium are not an accident. Without this industry, suicide bombers would not exist. They need their steady diet of hatred to survive.

And what is really shocking is the fact that decent, educated, honest people everywhere are not standing up against this campaign. The silent majority is very silent. No matter how shocking the anti-Israeli statements grow in Europe and the United States alike, no one stands up and says: "You are lying. You are deliberately spreading dangerous, vicious lies. Lies like these kill." The least we expect from decent people everywhere is to protest, to object, and to expose the lies.

If the campaign of lies bears fruits, it will not stop with Israel. Muslim minorities in Europe and in Russia can be expected to follow suit. The entire Western world will face a redoubled terror campaign—an infection they could have stopped before it spread throughout the world.

INTERMEZZO:
"THEY"

They started with the Jews. Their collapsing economy, their unemployment, and all the other failures of their society were blamed on the Jews. In moments of truth they declared that all the Jews should be eliminated. In more polite circumstances, they lamented that the Jews controlled the world, exploited the masses, and caused every agony. Their complaints were drawn from centuries of anti-Semitic literature.

They acquired the support of the masses through their fiery speeches, full of lies and fabrications. Their well-oiled propaganda machine was based on the principle that, if you repeated a lie often enough, the public would believe it. They used every possible weakness of democracy to gain political power and to achieve an aggressive military posture that began to endanger the world. Their most prominent religious authorities sometimes joined in, but certainly never tried to stop them.

At the beginning, Western Europe and America watched, but did nothing. After all, they weren't really involved. It was just the Jews. Not for the first time, a coalition of the anti-Semitic far Right and the pacifist and quasi-pacifist far Left explained that there was no need to fight—that war was a bad thing. "They don't really mean what they say," they reassured anyone who would listen. "We should take into account that they are poor, defeated, humiliated, and suffering."

Several countries became their allies. Others became silent supporters by omission or commission. Most of the Arab world cheered for them. At first even Soviet Russia helped them. As long as the Jews were the only victims, there were always excuses and explanations. No one boycotted them or removed them from the family of nations. International organizations did nothing to stop the madness.

Their power grew, but Western Europe embarked on an appeasement policy, never insisting on principles and begging for any minor concession. Although each new pact was trumpeted as a great achievement, the cost was always significant.

Finally the great conflict came. At the beginning they were successful. What they did to the Jews for years, they were now doing to others: Murdering civilians with no regard for the lives of women, children, and the elderly. It was sheer terror. But France could still not make up its mind whose side to take.

And then, like all ambitious evil leaders in the past, they and their allies made their big mistakes. Watching as Europe fell at their feet, they attacked both the United States and Russia. That was the beginning of their end. It took a few more years and much more blood, devastation, and agony. But the inevitable finally happened. They could not terrorize the entire world. They were badly defeated, and their own citizens paid dearly for the criminal ambitions of their leaders. They remained a dark chapter in the modern history of human horrors.

In case you were wondering, this was the story of Hitler and the Nazis. Does history repeat itself? Sometimes.

PART IV

THE UNCERTAIN FUTURE

—25—

THEY MEAN WHAT THEY SAY

If you pursue an evenhanded policy between the cat and the mouse, do you help the mouse to survive—or allow the cat to eat half of the mouse?

The conflict in the eye of the storm is definitely solvable. It's not difficult to envision how the Middle East would look after a fair resolution of the hundred-year-old Israeli-Palestinian dispute. But certain basic realities have to be understood by the world, and by the two sides, before any solution is achieved.

Conflicts between nations are abundant. They evolve around a variety of issues—from territorial and economic interests to natural resources, religion, and much else. We can trust the human race to find ample reasons for fighting and quarreling. The intensity and style of these conflicts have changed with time. When we talk today about "the civilized world," we're referring, among other things, to the will to solve problems through negotiation, compromise, patience, and financial arrangements, rather than the old habit of killing one another.

It is no accident that the word genocide is much more terrifying than the word war. There is a big difference between the annihilation of an entire population, an ethnic group, or a tribe, and a "normal" war, with all its casualties and traumas. For a crime to rise to the level of genocide, there must be intention, usually over a long period of time.

There is also a significant difference between a conflict over a specific territory and a conflict in which one side is aiming for the total annihilation of the other side. In the first case, negotiations and compromises are an option. In the second, they are not. In the first case, it's possible that each side is partly right and partly wrong. In the second, it is not.

If one nation intends to destroy another, to murder its population and eliminate the entity altogether, there's nothing left to discuss or compromise about. When Iran and the Palestinians talk openly about annihilating the state of Israel, what kind of compromise can we expect them to entertain? That they would settle for annihilating half of Israel? That only a quarter of the Jews must die?

Such demands to eliminate Israel can be heard at several different levels of Arab society. The most explicit policy is the one taken by the government of Iran, Hizbullah, Hamas, the Islamic Jihad, and assorted other Arab organizations. They, at least, are honest about this issue. Despite their frankness, however, the world does not believe them—much as they refused to believe Hitler when he announced his plans.

The mere fact that the government of Iran can make such statements and still have diplomatic or commercial relations with any civilized country is a disgrace to humanity. If Israel were militarily weaker, Europeans might already be attending academic conferences titled, "Could the Second Holocaust Have Been Avoided?" and Holocaust museums around the world might be forced to open new wings. Even writing such things might get a person dismissed as hysterical in some quarters. Why? Because the Israeli armed forces do not allow this to happen and the world doesn't want to hear it.

From time to time, I hear about European friends who deal or trade with these countries or groups. I know that these same people would be devastated if something terrible happened to me, my family, or my country. But they simply do not believe what they are explicitly told. Twenty-first-century Europeans have a hard time believing that someone wishes to annihilate an entire nation—much as, before 2003, they might have had a hard time believing that humanitarian aid workers and journalists might be kidnapped and beheaded.

There is a more sophisticated version of the explicit desire to destroy Israel. It is essentially the same idea as practiced by the mainstream Palestinians and many Arab states. It is the old charade of "the right of return," meaning the immigration of millions of Palestinians into Israel. Some claim that even if the Palestinians are offered the right to return, they will choose not to. Well, this might have been true if anyone would have lifted a finger during the past fifty-seven years to help them settle where they were. If they do not want to return, why aren't they settled in their current places?

We often hear about talk of Arab-sponsored peace plans—of a "just solution for the refugee problem" and of "the legitimate rights of the Palestinians." What this means, in practice, is the relocation of three million Palestinians into Israel. It is equivalent to demanding that two hundred million Mexicans move into the United States, except that no Mexican wants to kill all Americans and no Mexican wants to destroy the United States. It is equivalent to moving 40 million Algerians to France, except that no Algerian wants to destroy France. Somehow, this simple fact never comes up when reporters present their sound bites on the latest "peace" statement from the Arab League.

One Iranian Judo champion, who was a serious candidate for an Olympic medal in the Athens games, "refused to touch a Zionist athlete" and returned to Iran from Athens before competing. The president of Iran, allegedly representing the "moderate wing" of the regime, announced that Iran would consider the man a gold medalist. This is a stupid little story, but it tells a much larger story.

Whenever you read of any Arab leader presenting a new peace plan, always look for the fine print. If he refers to the "right of return," the peace he is talking about is the peace of a cemetery. If he refers to "Palestinian rights," confirm whether he means only a Palestinian state, which is fine and reasonable, or the "right of return," which is not. It is dispiriting how often politicians, Middle East experts, and journalists fail to perform even this trivial check on any such statement.

The Israeli-Palestinian conflict takes place on a number of levels. One level is entirely taken up with questions: Should there be an independent Palestinian state? Should Israel withdraw to the Green Line or to a compromise border? Should Syria get back the Golan Heights—all of it, most of it, or part of it? Should the Israeli settlements be dismantled? All of them? Some of them? None of them? Should the Arab parts of Jerusalem be in a Palestinian state—and, if so, which ones? Should there be any kind of financial arrangement for refugees on both sides? Should there be an exchange of territory? Should the Palestinian state be demilitarized—and, if so, what would that mean?

All of these are conventional issues, the kind most normal conflicts and even war situations are made of. All of them can be solved through negotiation, many of them through compromise. Others can be defused through creative solutions. As I argue later, most reasonable people have a very good idea of what the final arrangement should be; the only real unknowns are when this will occur and how much blood will be spilled before then.

But it is absolutely crucial to distinguish between the two levels of the dispute: the conventional level and the "annihilation level." One is negotiable; the other is not. One is a starter; the other is a nonstarter. The best thing the world can do to help make progress toward peace is to exclude from the family of nations anyone who even raises the possibility of annihilating Israel—however politely they do so. As long as this is on anyone's agenda, no progress can happen.

There are some naive people, even within Israel, who say that "the right of return" is the Palestinians' main bargaining chip, and they cannot be expected to abandon it before any serious negotiations begin. Any street-market merchant in the Middle East will tell you that a bargaining chip works only if it's something the other side might consider a possibility, however remote. The demand to destroy an entire country cannot be a bargaining chip. If you are negotiating the price of an Oriental rug, a threat to kill the customer cannot be a bargaining chip.

On the conventional level, it's legitimate to take an evenhanded approach or to conclude that one side or the other has valid arguments or grievances. Every opinion is open for debate; nothing is carved in stone. But when the question at hand is simply, "Shall we kill all the Israeli Jews or not?" being "evenhanded" will only result in continued tragedy in the region.

To be objective and to be evenhanded are two different things. If someone were to announce that Napoleon was Russian and that Japan was attacked by the Americans in Pearl Harbor, and a second person were to deny both allegations, an "evenhanded" observer might conclude that these were simply two versions of the same events. It takes an objective person to point out that the first man is lying.

—26—

WHY DON'T YOU CHOOSE
SOMEONE ELSE?

*In the universe, there is more matter than anti-matter. I wish I
could say the same about Semites.*

As a fifth generation Israeli, I grew up with no real understanding
of what anti-Semitism was all about. In my youth, I had never
seen an anti-Semitic person. All the people around me, good and
bad, were Jewish. They were generous or stingy, clever or stupid, dili-
gent or lazy, rich or poor—anything you wish. There were Jewish scientists, Jewish taxi drivers, Jewish prostitutes, and Jewish policemen.
The result fulfilled one of the dreams of the founding fathers of modern Israel: They wanted a normal society and they got it.

We did learn at school about two thousand years of persecution by
the Catholic Church, about the pogroms in Russia, and, above all,
about the Holocaust. But to us, young Israelis growing up in our own
country, these were topics from the history books, not realities. We also
knew that many Nobel laureates, outstanding musicians, and chess
champions were Jewish—but we also knew that by and large the Jews
were a very small group on the world scene. The total number of Jews in

the entire world is smaller than the number of people in either Istanbul or Mexico City. Yet somehow we are always in the news.

Many years later, at a fund-raising dinner in the United States for an Israeli institute of scientific research, the guest of honor was a Catholic cardinal. The host, a local rabbi, wanted to praise his ecumenism, tolerance, and friendship. "I hereby appoint you an honorary Jew," he announced good-naturedly. "This entitles you to two thousand years of retroactive persecution."

Having traveled the world as a scientist, I have not personally experienced more examples of anti-Semitism than I have examples of anti-French or anti-German feelings. But there is a clear revival of anti-Semitism in Europe, arguably dominated partly—but not only—by incited young Muslims. Books and essays, doctorates and debates, have been devoted to the subject. As an Israeli by birth and residence, I do not qualify to add anything profound to this debate.

But I do know certain facts. It has been a tradition in the UN General Assembly that the Irish delegation proposes an annual resolution against all kinds of racism. It is a fact that anti-Semitism has not been included in the condemned list. Why? Perhaps it is because a very large number of UN member states believe there is nothing wrong with anti-Semitism. I assume that the EU countries are not of this opinion. But how could they compromise on such an issue? Would they agree to exclude racism against black people from such a resolution because fifty white supremacist nations would threaten to vote against it? I find this truly unbelievable.

When Israel demanded that Ireland change the text of the resolution, the Irish first agreed—only to retreat in response to Arab pressure. It is gratifying, but sad, that only in November 2004 did Europe insist on including anti-Semitism on the list of censured acts. Facing a resolute European stand, the Arabs did not dare vote against the resolution.

Most of Globania has never heard this story. Who cares about such resolutions? They have little effect on actual racism in the world; their value, if any, is largely symbolic. But there are certain things one should never compromise about, especially in symbolic issues. Europe is too eager to compromise on such issues, which are matters of life and death for entire nations — or, rather, for one entire nation.

This is not an isolated incident. The infamous UN Durban conference in South Africa a few years ago made a strong point of not accepting anti-Semitism as a form of discrimination. Again, it's hardly surprising that the Arabs and most Muslim countries should support such a thing. But Europe, with its history, should never compromise on such matters — unless somewhere, deep in its heart, it still carries the deadly virus.

It was equally unbelievable when the French ambassador to London, at a social evening attended by many influential people, referred to Israel as "that shitty little country," explaining that most of the troubles of the world would disappear if Israel did not exist. The French Foreign Ministry issued no denial or reprimand in the wake of the incident — again, hardly an isolated case of European anti-Semitism.

Can you oppose Israeli policy without being anti-Semitic? Of course. I am a living example. Can you oppose settlements in the West Bank without being labeled anti-Semitic? Absolutely. Can you wish that all Israelis be annihilated without being anti-Semitic? I don't think so. Can you applaud the murder of Jewish children who are killed by suicide bombers, just because they are Jewish, without being anti-Semitic? Well, what do you think?

The Palestinians claim that their problem is not with the Jews, but with Israel. Yet years ago, when they hijacked the Air France flight from Athens to Paris and took it to Entebbe, they released all the non-Jewish passengers and kept all the Jews, even if they were French or Greek. When they attacked synagogues in Paris and Tunis, they weren't acting against Israel. When a Palestinian suicide murderer boarded a bus in Galilee and noticed two Israeli Arab women sitting in the bus, he told them to get off at the next stop and only then blew himself up, killing numerous Jewish passengers. He made a very clear distinction between killing innocent Israelis and killing innocent Jews. He chose the latter. When Jewish cemeteries in Europe are covered with graffiti and swastikas almost daily and their tombstones are broken by vandals, this is not an act against a country but against a people.

On the conventional level of the Arab-Israeli dispute, anyone in the world is entitled to his or her own opinion, and no one has the right to label such a view as anti-Semitic purely to score emotional points. But the simple goal of killing Jews just because they are Jews and destroying Israel cannot be part of that conventional dialogue. Anyone who takes such a position is anti-Semitic by definition. If advocating the killing of all Israeli Jews is not anti-Semitism, what is?

The question is: Which issues belong to which category? If you oppose Israeli settlements, if you think that a Palestinian state is overdue, or if you believe that killing the leaders of terrorists is not an effective method, you may be right or you may be wrong, but those positions shouldn't get you condemned as an anti-Semite.

However, if you blow up a synagogue in Istanbul or a Jewish community center in Buenos Aires, there's nothing to discuss. If you believe that Israel has no right to defend itself against murders and against shelling, while every other nation has the right of self-defense, there's nothing to discuss. If you help directly or indirectly to finance terrorist organizations whose declared goal is to kill all Jews, there's nothing to discuss. If you hold an international conference on women and child trafficking and the only country condemned is Israel, there's nothing to discuss. And if you propose resolutions that outlaw any form of racism except anti-Semitism, chances are pretty good that you're anti-Semitic.

The Arabs have repeatedly claimed that Israel is using accusations of anti-Semitism as a propaganda weapon. This reminds me of a story: In a large square in Mexico City, two beggars sat next to each other. One had a plate marked with a cross. The other had a plate marked with a Star of David. One after the other, the people who passed ignored the Star of David and threw coin after coin into the plate with the cross. After a while, a priest passed by and noticed that the beggar with the Star of David had an empty plate. "Son," he said, "Mexico is a Catholic country. Perhaps it would help if you would remove the sign from your plate." The beggar looked at his friend and said, "Moishe, he is trying to teach us how to run our business."

Of course Jews sometimes try to raise sympathy by crying anti-Semitism. But every Jew would be happy to give up this option if the plague of anti-Semitism finally vanished from the earth.

When a Jew heard from his rabbi that the Jews were "the chosen people," he raised his head to heaven and asked, "Dear God, why don't you choose someone else?"

—27—

MILLI-GLOBANIA IN THE
EYE OF THE STORM

Where else can you find a country with strong ties to the United States, an elaborate association agreement with the European Union, a large Arab minority, and a population in which every sixth person was educated in Russia?

Globania has more than six billion people. Israel has more than six million. Globania has more than a billion Muslims. Israel has more than a million. Globania probably has an additional billion or more truly religious people of various levels of fundamentalism. Israel has an additional million or more. Globania has close to a billion people who were recently released from the claws of communism. Israel has a million immigrants from the former Soviet Union. Israel accounts for roughly one-thousandth of Globania. You might call it a little Milli-Globania.

To be a true Milli-Globania, Israel should produce one-thousandth of the world's gross product, one-thousandth of its scientific research, one-thousandth of its literature, and one-thousandth of its HIV-positive cases. Instead, its GDP is four times larger, its scientific output is ten times larger, and its HIV-positive rate is minuscule. On many other grounds—its tendency to dominate the news, the unfortunate sanctity of numerous sites, the emotional level of the conflicts, and the sheer human variation to be found on its streets—Israel boasts probably the highest rates in the world.

Israel is small and dry. If Finland is the land of a thousand lakes, Israel is the land of two, and one of them is dead. Israel's most famous river, the Jordan, would be considered a creek in most other countries. At its narrowest point, discounting the West Bank, the width of Israel can be traversed in ten minutes—by car, not by plane. At its widest, it is as large as the distance from London to Oxford, or from the southern edge of Washington to the northern end of Baltimore.

Israel is densely populated—much more than the average density of Globania, but not as densely as the Netherlands, Belgium, or Japan. But this Milli-Globania has many demographic similarities to Globania. The less affluent and the very religious Israelis, both Jews and Arabs, have a very high birthrate and natural population growth. This is an intrinsic time bomb. It means that the nation is due for a growing number of children in poverty, a decreasing average education level due to lack of family resources, a smaller percentage of knowledge-rich workers, and a long-term decline. As in Globania, the growing social gaps—rather than the ongoing effects of terrorism—are, in the long run, the nation's most important problem. And the solution is similarly tedious: education, education, and education.

The annual GDP of Israel, more than $100 billion, comes to an average of roughly $17,000 per capita. Only twenty-five countries in the world exceed this number. And when you exclude from the calculation the ultraorthodox Jewish community and the Arab community, both of which produce much less than the average and have many more children, it becomes clear that the remainder of the country produces almost as much per capita as the richest European countries.

Milli-Globania is in the eye of the Middle Eastern storm, but the storm is much wider. A huge number of problems are concentrated in a small speck. Making one nation out of a million or more Arabs, a million or more orthodox Jews, a million or so Russian immigrants, and three million others whose families have been in the area any-where between fifty and two hundred years is quite a task.

Israelis can be very warm people, but they are also the product of permanent danger and tension. Things like politeness, good driving habits, standing in line, and obeying rules are not the Israelis' strong suits. If creativity is one of Israel's national assets, chaos, of one sort or another, is one of its standard features. Being considerate to others is not the norm, except at times of real danger, when the nation becomes a united tribe, if not a family.

Israelis use words from the Bible when they shop in the supermar-ket. The words for bread, milk, meat, veal, and fish; for buying and selling; and for paying and traveling are the same ones used by King David in Jerusalem three thousand years ago. At the same time, many contemporary Israelis have learned Hebrew from their children, who learned it in school or in the street. Hebrew was resurrected as a living language in the nineteenth century; it is probably the oldest language to have its own new word for a taxi, derived from a biblical root. My late grandfather Haim Harari was the first teacher of Hebrew grammar and literature at Gymnasia Herzlia, the first Hebrew high school in the world, founded in Jaffa in 1905. Both my parents had Hebrew as their mother tongue; both, like me, graduated from this school.

Given that most Israeli families are refugees from countries that have never enjoyed democracy—either in Eastern Europe or in the Arab world—the rough and wild Israeli democracy is amazing. But Is-rael has also seen a Jew murder one of its prime ministers and has oth-ers who refuse to serve in a conquering army or serve in an army that must evacuate Jewish settlements. It has right-wing extremists who are as bad as any in the world and left-wing extremists who can be de-scribed only as anti-Semitic Jews.

But there is also an excellent hard core of truly idealistic people. They love their country; believe in democracy; make great contribu-tions to art, culture, and science; serve as creative, brave, and loyal sol-diers and officers; build a fantastic high-tech industry; create a thriving economy; and will do anything for peace except commit national or personal suicide. These are the people who carry the country on their shoulders except when their own coffins are carried on the shoulders of their friends.

Israel has always suffered physically, yet been enriched intellectually, because of its geographic location at the crossroads of three continents. In a time of peace, however, the eye of the storm and the crossroads of the continents could become a jewel. Israel could never dominate the Arab world, even if it wanted to—it is too small for that—but it could be a central source of economic development for the entire region. Far better than other countries—including Turkey—Israel could serve as a bridge between the Middle East and Europe. Israel has a great relationship with the United States, a close kinship to Europe, a significant Russian-speaking population, and a large Arab minority. If that isn't the ideal blueprint for a bridge between cultures, styles, languages, and religions, what is?

An Israel at peace with its neighbors could truly be a Milli-Globania: a miniature of the good and the bad of the world, a laboratory for solving human problems, and a hub of communication, art, culture, and transportation. Is this pure fantasy? Not at all. Will any of us live to see it? I doubt it.

Yet if we, the people of Globania, had any sense, we could make it happen.

In the meantime, how symbolic it is that Israel and the Arabs share the lowest point on Earth, the Dead Sea. It would take a relatively small hill of four hundred meters (1,300 feet) to bring it to sea level, but it is not easy to do.

—28—

COLLECTIVE SUICIDE

A society that produces suicide murderers in quantity is essentially committing suicide.

From September 11 in the United States to the numerous suicide bombings in Iraq, Russian suicides originating in Chechnya, sporadic events in other countries, and the Palestinian terror in Israel, the suicide murder has become the trademark of Islamic terrorism in our time. But there is another suicidal tendency that accompanies these acts, which is even more devastating. This tendency is the collective suicide of entire Muslim communities or nations at the hands of leaders who drive them into self-destruction.

The Shiites are the majority in Iraq. They were persecuted and powerless under Saddam Hussein, who murdered them in huge numbers without the slightest hesitation. It was always clear that any democratically or even quasi-democratically elected regime in Iraq would give them dominant influence at one level or another. It is equally clear that Iran, the perennial enemy of Iraq, is interested in a foothold within its neighbor, if not in completely controlling it. Iran's simplest way of gaining influence or control in Iraq is via its Shiite community. Major factions of the Iraqi Shiites behave as if their top priority is to prevent any democratization and to bring into Iraq a dominating Iranian influence—never realizing, apparently, that they will be the first victims of such a development.

The Saudi regime is a major target of Osama bin Laden and his friends. This fact does not stop the Saudis from heavily financing the outer circle of religious-based incitement, which serves as the infrastructure for most Islamic terrorism. It is obvious that, sooner or later, the Saudi regime will be a major victim, through a chain reaction, of its own global blindness.

Iran could live peacefully and exploit its abundant natural resources to advance its population. For the past few generations, no one has threatened Iran from the outside—except Saddam, who is gone, thanks to the hated Americans. Instead Iran has become the number one terrorist state, with global ambitions. Its attempts to develop nuclear weapons and to manage subsidiary terror networks far away from home with a general policy that can lead to a short-term failure or to temporary success followed by devastating long-term results for itself.

Jordan is another suicidal nation. In 1967, when Israel was engaged on two fronts with Egypt and Syria, Jordan could have emerged as a regional power had it stayed out of the war. Instead, King Hussein believed the lies of Egypt's President Nasser, who claimed rousing victories even after his air force was completely destroyed. Hussein was dragged by Nasser into attacking Jerusalem and other areas, finally losing the West Bank, which Israel hadn't even dreamed of conquering. Following 1967, King Hussein hosted Arafat and the PLO, only to fall victim to their attempts to destroy Jordan and to murder him, culminating in the expulsion of Arafat in 1970. In 1991, King Hussein was one of very few Arab rulers who supported Saddam, losing important points in the eyes of his American protectors.

Finally, the Palestinians. They are the world champions in self-inflicted tragedies. In the 1930s, the British offered them a partition of Palestine, giving the Jews only a small part of the area. Yet the Palestinians rejected the offer, choosing instead to support the Nazis against the British. In 1947, they were offered an independent state that would take up half of Palestine. Once again, they rejected the offer, attacked, and lost almost everything. In the 1950s and 1960s, they could have achieved a certain degree of autonomy under Jordan and Egypt. Instead they attacked Israel sporadically. For years, they could have settled their refugees, who lived in poverty. Instead they allowed two generations to perish in their own self-confining camps and perpetuated the misery of their own people—simply to try to destroy another people who refused to be destroyed.

In Oslo, the Palestinians signed an agreement that gave them control of major parts of their area—a move designed as a stepping stone to more autonomy. Some measure of economic development and cooperation followed. At President Bill Clinton's Camp David summit, they were offered parts of Jerusalem and almost all of the West Bank and Gaza. It is not entirely clear whether the Israeli public would have accepted this offer, but the Palestinians rejected the plan, again insisting on the infamous "right of return."

The current intifada is the ultimate suicidal exercise. If you're trying to damage a country or convince it to yield a point or two in some dispute, the use of aggression, terror, and war might have an impact. But you cannot use terror and murder to convince a whole country to disappear. It was entirely clear, from the first minute, that by pushing Israel with such a sequence of atrocities, the Palestinians were bringing yet another calamity on themselves. How else could Israel react? How else would anybody react?

As a result, the Palestinians have succeeded in politically destroying the Israeli left, which lost half of its power in the elections after the Israeli public realized that Arafat was interested only in the destruction of Israel after all. It is simply not possible to pursue a peace-loving policy when your supermarket, your favorite restaurant, and the bus taking your children to school are likely to explode at any moment. Arafat himself did everything possible to convince the world of his intentions through his deeds and his duplicity. The Americans, who served as an honest broker for many years, were essentially forced by Arafat to declare him irrelevant. They finally caught him in a sequence of such blatant lies that they could no longer overlook what the world should have understood long ago: The man was incapable of speaking the truth.

Whether this situation will change in the post-Arafat era, we have yet to see.

Europe is not entirely blameless in the plight of the Palestinian. The Palestinian leader who destroyed his people again and again, who tried to murder King Hussein, who destroyed Lebanon in a civil war, who killed the Israeli athletes in the Munich Olympics was received and embraced by the Pope (whom he must have told that Jesus was Palestinian) and by every other European leader. Israel itself is not free of blame; after all, the Oslo agreements, which all moderate and left-of-center Israelis (including me) supported, proved to be an invitation for the next round of violence rather than a step toward peace.

Even within their current disaster, the Palestinians continue to do everything possible to destroy their own people and their own community. When Israel opens crossing points to allow Palestinians to go to work in Israel, they blow them up, causing a few Israeli casualties but increasing the misery of thousands of their own brothers. When they use hospitals and ambulances for terror, they endanger the lives of the genuinely sick and wounded, who must be checked carefully and delayed. When Israel built an industrial zone on the border of the Gaza Strip to provide employment and economic cooperation, the Palestinians repeatedly blew up the various businesses, forcing Israel to close the zone and increasing unemployment in Gaza. The list never ends.

Eventually more and more Palestinians began to understand what their leadership had done to them. But they were unable to oppose it, and the incitement continued. Step by step they are losing everything, and they show no signs of being able to stop. The corruption of the leading figures in the Palestinian authority is dramatic, even by the standards of the Arab world. The wife and daughter of Arafat have been happily deposited in Paris with a huge monthly allowance, paid by the allegedly bankrupt Palestinian authority; the suicide murderers of the Al Aksa brigade are financed from the same pockets, though they still deny it. The fight to control Arafat's legendary bank accounts has just begun.

The post-Arafat Palestinian leadership is beginning to understand the situation. Within twenty-four hours after Arafat's death, they succeeded in stopping most terror attacks in Gaza, proving to the world that all the claims that Arafat was unable to stop terror were blatant lies.

At the personal level of the honest, hard-working, peaceful Palestinian, this is a profound tragedy. Such people are prevented from starting a new life by their own leadership, which wants them to remain refugees. They are denied work by their own countrymen. They live in shameful poverty while their leaders indulge. Their children do not always go to school, while many of the leaders' children attend private schools in Europe. They are told twice a day that all of their troubles are due to the American criminals and the Zionist aggressors, but they cannot feed and educate their children with such statements. They are never told that part of their misery stems from the fact that certain enlightened countries still support their corrupt leaders with the single-minded goal of destroying Israel.

In a way, the real tragedy is this: Everybody knows that the Palestinians have only two options—peace or further calamity. Everybody knows that, when peace comes, its main features will be no surprise. The Palestinians can win only by halting terror, abandoning the wish to destroy Israel, and trying to press for a true peace. Will they continue to destroy themselves and make others suffer? Time will tell.

—29—

EVERYBODY KNOWS
THE SOLUTION

*The unsolvable problems have clear solutions, but no one knows
how to solve the solvable ones.*

One day there will be peace in the Middle East. No one knows
when this day will come, or just what will happen before it arrives. But most thinking people know, more or less, what form it
will have. It may happen within a few years or a few decades. It may be
preceded by one or more future wars or simply by continued terror and
agitation. But peace will almost certainly come.

There are certain immutable facts in the Middle East. Peace can arrive only if the Palestinians accept the existence of Israel. Peace can materialize only if the Palestinians have their own state—next to Israel, not
instead of it. The densely Jewish areas will be part of Israel; the densely
Palestinian areas will be part of the Palestinian state. Israel will have an
Arab minority. Many Israeli settlements in the West Bank and Gaza will
have to be abandoned. Most of Jerusalem will remain in Israel, and it
will continue to be the capital city. Some heavily populated Arab neighborhoods of the greater Jerusalem area will be in the Palestinian state and
may form its capital city. A carefully planned demilitarization strategy

must be developed; it will take a substantial number of years and can be lifted only by mutual consent. Descendents of Palestinian refugees will be settled in Arab countries, many of them in the Palestinian state. All Arab countries bordering with Israel will have peace agreements with it, and no unresolved territorial disputes will remain. The borders between Israel and its Arab neighbors will be protected by some kind of fence, even if the two sides love each other, if only because no open border can survive a 20:1 income ratio.

All of these conclusions are inevitable—not because everybody accepts them today, but because all sides must accept them before peace can be achieved. If any one of them fails to materialize, peace in the region will remain elusive. These measures reflect the wishes of a clear majority in Israel, although there will continue to be fierce resistance from an influential minority. As yet there is no majority support for such measures among the Palestinians, but it is not clear that such a majority matters because at the moment their democracy is more virtual than real. In any case, without a decision by the Palestinian leadership to replace terror and follow such a program, nothing can happen. We do not know how many years will pass and how much bloodshed there will be before peace arrives, simply because we do not know how and when everybody will finally accept the preceding conclusions.

It is paradoxical that all of these issues, which are the most difficult and the most contested elements of the conflict, have unique and clear answers. It is just a matter of time until everyone comes to accept them. But if all of this is true, what are the remaining questions? Quite a few items remain, but almost none are as important (or as controversial) as the preceding list.

The exact boundary between Israel and the Palestinian state will be little different from the Green Line, but the two will not be identical. Whether Israel will include 3 or 5 or 10 or 20 percent of the area of the West Bank remains to be seen, but even so everybody knows which areas are candidates for inclusion in Israel. We do not know if the Palestinian state will include areas that are in Israel today, but if so, they can only be empty land in the corner of the Negev or densely populated Israeli Arab areas near the Green Line. We do not know which part of the greater Jerusalem area will be in Palestinian hands, but the possibilities are limited. We do not know what shape the relation will take between the Palestinian state and Jordan, which has a clear Palestinian majority. They may be totally separate, united in a confederation, or even merged. We do not know what type of demilitarization plan will be agreed on, but it must allow that no one in the Palestinian state has the option to start any new conflict. All of these questions leave room for negotiation, but they all fall into the category of "conventional conflict" and fall short of the prospect of annihilation.

A few issues remain, though they are truly minor. One is the division of water resources—an issue that's minor because drought will eventually force both sides to desalinate water, reducing the problem to a question of money. There are issues of Palestinian access to the Mediterranean and free passage between Gaza and the rest of the Palestinian state. These issues can be solved in many different ways and will cease to be an issue if peace is real.

The preceding issues are divided into two groups. All the truly difficult issues have clear and specific solutions, without which there cannot be peace, no matter what anyone believes or says. They are all nonnegotiable. There will not be peace without two states, without settled refugees in Arab countries, without dismantling settlements, and without the other mandatory elements listed earlier.

All the easier issues offer plenty of room for negotiation and compromise. They are all painted in shades of gray, not black or white.

It is an amazing situation. All that's left is for the parties involved to accept the terms of the obvious resolution. In a way, these problems have already been solved; it's just that no leaders have yet stepped forward to embrace the solutions. However, the solvable questions will require further debate—although this can happen only after the long-disputed basic problems have been resolved.

This is the crazy Middle East at its very best: The insolvable problems have been solved, but no one knows it. The solvable problems have not been solved, and no one knows the solutions.

The only remaining problem is one that I have deliberately left for the end, as it should be among the leaders themselves: the Old City of Jerusalem. Sometimes I suspect that this city is the ultimate proof that there is no God. When I see the amount of trouble that this one square kilometer of real estate has brought on Jews, Christians, and Muslims over so many centuries, I can't help feeling that if there were a God, he would have found a way to evacuate, unite, or destroy this place so that human beings would stop killing one another over it. (And if God did not exist, there would be no reason for such fuss over a holy site!)

There it is: another crazy Middle Eastern paradox.

Unfortunately, the problem is much more serious than any silly games of logic can address. The ultimate status of the Temple Mount is one problem with no clear solution. The only way to handle the disposition may be to leave it to the very end of the dispute, after everything else has been settled and after old enemies have kissed and made up.

Perhaps this analysis may seem oversimplified, even somewhat naive. Yet I truly believe that the broad lines of the ultimate peace agreement are clear to nearly everyone. Only those involved remain in the dark.

—30—

THE NUCLEAR STONE AGE

You cannot punish a suicide murderer by death penalty. You cannot bomb into the Stone Age someone who is already there.

The new, undeclared World War III against Islamic terror and its numerous manifestations is the big storm of our time. It has a life of its own, regardless of when and how the Israeli-Palestinian conflict, in the eye of the storm, is solved.

The two sides that fought in World War I lived in the same century, but in different places. The same is true for World War II. In World War III, both sides are almost everywhere, but they live in different centuries.

The atrocities performed by the Islamic terrorists would appear much less shocking if they were observed with the help of a time machine, taking us back to, say, 1850. Before the modern era of warfare, killing women, children, and the elderly deliberately and without any apparent reason was a normal wartime practice. There was no adherence to any international law. Suicide murders, beheadings, the mutilation of dead bodies, holding children as hostages, and other such acts would hardly raise an eyebrow. Religious incitement, based on absurd lies, was standard operating procedure. Using medical installations, schools, and places of worship as bases of operation would not create an outrage. Civil rights for women were almost unheard of. To declare that the followers of a certain religion were outcasts or inferior human beings was not only acceptable but also common.

Saudi Arabia, where women are considered subhuman and stoning is still an accepted punishment, is largely financing our modern trip back to the nineteenth century. Afghanistan, where women were treated even worse than in Saudi Arabia, served as the basis for one active component of this effort. Iran, a theocracy that would have fit naturally into the nineteenth century, is enriching uranium, but it's not enriching much else except international terror.

Of course, we do not live in 1850, or 1900 or even 1940. Nevertheless, the terrorists are using the technology of today to try to drag us back to the distant past. Satellite TV, exploding airplanes, Internet incitement, and the rapid movement of huge sums of money from continent to continent weren't available in the past, but today they are being used by the planners of this voyage back in time.

There are much more lethal technologies on the agenda. Chemical weapons, standard in World War I, have been unacceptable ever since. This didn't stop the Egyptians from using them against Yemen in the 1960s, Saddam from murdering the Kurds with them in the 1980s, or, according to some reports, Sudan from trying them recently with its genocidal campaign against its black citizens. Nothing stops the intercontinental terror networks from using chemical weapons against anyone they do not like—whether it's the French, with their law against head scarves, or the Australians, who are among the coalition forces in Iraq. The Palestinians, never to be last in this competition, have planned several times to poison the water systems of Israeli cities.

The same goes for biological weapons, which thankfully have not yet been used in warfare. No one has announced any findings concerning the Anthrax scare that followed September 11, but it only reminded us that the possibility of such weapons exists—and, in spite of a major defensive and therapeutic effort, the Western world is not really prepared to handle such attacks. Modern biotechnology offers sobering possibilities for people sufficiently evil and knowledgeable to contemplate using such things to harm others.

The use of radioactive materials for creating "dirty bombs" is as easy as anything can be. These are not nuclear weapons, which explode with the energy of the sun; their danger is considerably smaller, but their public impact could be enormous. Such a bomb could be produced with normal, even homemade, explosives. Radioactive materials, of the kind available in any hospital, could be added to the standard cocktail of nails and metal fragments used by all the Palestinian and Iraqi suicide murderers; the result would cause much more death and irreversible injury. It seems that the real reason such weapons have not yet been used is that the experts who can handle such materials are unwilling to sacrifice themselves and the expendable suicide bombers are unable to deal with such technology. This situation, however, could change at any time.

Finally, there is the nuclear option, with its potential to take us back almost to the Stone Age. We should remember that nuclear weapons manufacture is a sixty-year-old technology. Almost every country can produce an automobile, a TV set, or an airplane to the standards of the 1940s. Nuclear weapons are no exception. All that's needed is a modicum of knowledge, a basic technological capability, crucial materials, money, and the will to go ahead. A small group of terrorists might not be able to do it on their own, but a country that hosts terrorists and supports them could do it relatively easily.

The main problem with a potential Iranian nuclear weapon is that it would make Iran nearly untouchable as its leaders proceeded to expand their global terror campaign. Iran already operates far from its borders, manipulating and directing numerous terror organizations, both visible and invisible. All it needs, as a terrorist state, is an insurance policy. Global terror, with a friendly home base, protected by a nuclear umbrella, is the wet dream of any terror leader.

Another major problem with an Iranian nuclear program is that it would induce other Islamic programs. The world is concerned about Islamic terror, but there have been many wars and conflicts between Muslim countries. An Iranian bomb could induce Saudi Arabia, Kuwait,

Syria, Egypt, Algeria, Libya, and Kazakhstan to initiate their own nuclear programs.

For several decades, the world has talked about an Israeli nuclear capability. The fact is that, throughout all the wars of these decades, nothing of the sort has ever been used, and no one has even threatened to use it. If such a capability exists, then, it can hardly pose much of a threat to anyone. If it did, even as a deterrent, we would have heard such statements from Israel long ago.

A war between different centuries, fought all around the globe, is very different from a war fought in one place among enemies living in the same century. You can't destroy the economy of someone who has no real economy. You can't threaten a suicide murderer with the death penalty. You can't bomb into the Stone Age someone who is already there. You can't bring yourself to forget all the rules and moral standards gained in the past hundred years to fight an undeclared war against an enemy who has never heard of these rules. You can't win a soccer match against a team that uses its hands and refuses to accept any penalty.

To win any war, you have to gain the upper hand at both the tactical and the strategic levels. At the tactical level, the answer is clear, although many have not yet internalized it. The only way to win the war on terrorism is to mount an aggressive, offensive war, without any compromise, against the terrorists, their supporters, and their shelters.

The strategic level is a completely different story. The ultimate strategic weapon in such a war is to deplete the human reservoir of people of the other side. This does not mean killing anyone. It means bringing the potential supporters of terror from the nineteenth century into our time. We don't have a century or more to accomplish this. It must be done energetically, passionately, and soon.

Not everything is perfect in our time, of course. But we cannot go back selectively in time. We cannot maintain our life of good health, democracy, equality, human rights, intellectual challenges, and economic progress, while trying to regain some obscure phantom positive values of the nineteenth century, if they ever really existed. Remember, those who would go back to live in the trees or caves do so without benefit of antibiotics, toothpaste, eyeglasses, books, or cell phones.

Some might consider my attitude paternalistic. Others might think it smacks of nostalgia for colonialism. Neither claim is true. No one would wish a return to the days of the Indian and Iraqi civil service, when the British colonialists behaved as if they were higher life forms than the "natives" they presumed to govern. As one born in the British Empire in the Palestine mandate, I have absolutely no longing for those days.

In the same way that everything else has changed in the past century, there must also be new ways to bring people forward by education. Finding such ways and using them to bring billions of our fellow human beings forward are crucial to the survival of our planet. These are the dominant, long-term strategic weapons of the present war, and efforts to develop them should be at least as intensive as the efforts to develop the major strategic weapon of World War II. In the nuclear Stone Age, we need education to bridge the gap and to suppress the storm.

—31—

A CORRECT DIAGNOSIS IS
HALF A CURE

If, when evening comes, it is too dark to see what is happening, perhaps it's time to remove your sunglasses.

There once was a man who was a heavy drinker for thirty years. Ultimately, he was diagnosed with liver disease. "Well, no wonder he was drinking," his friends said with false wisdom. "That kind of deadly disease could drive anyone to drink."

Yasir Arafat initiated, led, and financed the modern wave of Palestinian terrorism. Some Palestinian policemen ended up as active murderers. Others literally displayed their hands dipped in the blood of murdered Israelis. Members of the Palestinian security forces moonlight as Hamas killers; their buildings often serve as terror bases. Neither Arafat nor the Palestinian forces under his command lifted a finger to curtail the terror. Finally Israel destroyed much of their infrastructure. "They cannot put an end to Palestinian terror because Israel has destroyed their capabilities," declared countless prominent American and European editorials. How interesting! And I always thought confusing cause and effect was a childhood phenomenon.

But now the lie has been exposed: When Arafat repeatedly announced that he condemned terror but could not stop it, most of the world believed him. When his successor stopped the terrorist activities almost immediately, everybody applauded. I have not seen one article pointing out that this instant improvement only proved that Arafat had been fooling the world for years. Surely at least some of the columnists who seconded Arafat's claims so forcefully might have stood up and admitted their mistake.

The global terror conglomerate cynically exploits every right, every privilege, and every sacred cow that a modern, democratic society can offer. The first step toward dismantling this network must be to recognize this fact. Unfortunately, many countries—especially in Europe— have yet to understand it. But it's difficult to cure a disease without a correct diagnosis.

Nations that fund, shelter, or guide major terror organizations must be identified and totally excluded from the family of nations. There is no other way. Engaging them in dialogue only lends credibility to their cause, while the murders continue.

There can be little doubt about these countries; every intelligence organization in the Western world knows exactly who they are. How can there be the slightest doubt about what Iran, Syria, and the Palestinians are doing today any more than there was about what Afghanistan, Iraq, and Libya were doing in the past? Don't we all know what the Saudis are funding?

In a conventional war, each country must identify itself as one of the fighting parties or as a neutral noncombatant. Global terrorism offers a much more comfortable option: You can have your cake and eat it, too, leading one of the camps in a global war and murdering thousands of innocents while denying that you have anything to do with it. That the world accepts such duplicity is incredible.

Arafat was the commander of the Fatah movement for more than thirty-five years. He was clearly in control of their actions. The movement sent suicide murderers—men and women alike—to kill civilians in Israeli streets, buses, and shops. The ubiquitous Saeb Erakat, Arafat's sidekick, condemned the crimes on every TV screen in the world—in English, but never in Arabic. Arafat himself mumbled something in English about not hurting civilians and then recommended in Arabic that more "martyrs" should join the ranks. He also financed the same murders he had just condemned. The entire world observed these actions, but some of its leaders continued to talk to Arafat, visit him, and consider him a suitable partner for further dialogue. Why?

Hizbullah runs a state within a state in Lebanon and occupies a large part of the country, including a flourishing drug production business. The organization is entirely under the control of Iran and is supplied, in broad daylight, through Syria. It is clearly a terrorist organization. Its links to other components of the international terror consortium are becoming clearer and clearer. There is not one government in the Western world that does not recognize these links. Why, then, do they still trade and communicate with Iran and Syria? Is it not clear that much of the Shiite terror in Iraq is fully funded and supported by Iran? Is there any question that Iran is trying to build nuclear capabilities in order to have immunity against international pressure?

Saudi Arabia funds a huge number of Islamic organizations, which are the fertile grounds from which terror is born and nurtured, from Manila, Kuala Lumpur, and Jakarta to London, Hamburg, and Rome, and especially in the Middle East. Why have the Saudis never received a clear ultimatum from the free world concerning this behavior?

These remarks may sound like the charges of a self-righteous Israeli who wants to settle accounts with the enemy. But the reach of Arab terror has by this point far exceeded the Middle East, to high-profile acts in New York, Madrid, Baghdad, Bali, Istanbul, Moscow, Yemen, Lockerby, Riyadh, Buenos Aires, Tunis, Washington, Nairobi, and places all over the world. These acts have emanated from one version or another of the terror conglomerate, which is financed, motivated, and propelled by the same countries. How can terror be stopped without eliminating the seeds of the poison plants and the heads of the snakes?

The Arab satellite TV channels, broadcast from relatively peaceful Arab countries such as Qatar, are gasoline poured daily on the fire of the terrorists. Why are they allowed to continue? The Al-Manar network, which belongs to Hizbullah, broadcasts venom to the entire Arabic-speaking world without interruption, using European and Saudi satellite services. When will the world understand that free speech and free religious practices go hand in hand with law and order, a judicial system, and democracy? You cannot pick and choose the features of the free world that help protect you while you kill people, and then expect to evade the consequences of a just society. A free country does offer free media access but also limits to racial incitement and libelous defamation. It's a package deal.

Terrorists who operate within a given country are criminals, and should be treated as such by the police and the courts. They are entitled to basic civil rights, like any other murderer. But terrorists who operate under the protection of another country must be declared by international law to be legitimate targets for any attack. And anyone who commands them, finances their activities, or shelters them should be treated the same way. And they cannot insist that they are innocent until proven guilty: That principle applies only to those who come to court and are subject to arrest, not to those who hide far beyond the reach of the law, protected by sovereign governments who deny their existence.

Before we can begin to discuss how the problem of international terror must be treated, we are first confronted with a major problem of diagnosis. In this case, as with much of medicine, a correct diagnosis is at least half a cure. Life-threatening diseases are commonly ignored by patients because their symptoms appear relatively benign. Denial is a well-known problem in medicine; the world may be sick, but it pretends it can be cured by faith healers.

Denial cannot work. The only thing that will is drastic treatment.

To switch metaphors: If you're confronted with a large barren area infested with poisonous scorpions, you have two methods of dealing with the problem. It's wise to use both methods. In the short term, the most efficient way is to eliminate the scorpions ruthlessly. In the long run, the only way is to cultivate the barren area and make it bloom. Both of these activities require determination and consistency.

Once the diagnosis is in place, the treatment is clear. Any proverbial taxi driver knows what needs to be done. The treatment doesn't require great scientific ability, and it's guaranteed to succeed. Here is the prescription: Declare the relevant countries as terrorist states; exclude them from interaction with the free world; seek out the terrorists themselves and destroy them wherever they are, including inside the terrorist states; block the flow of funds to organizations that incite to hatred and murder; trace the sources of funding of the nongovernmental organizations that are secretly funded by terror-related sources; apply consistent strong pressure in favor of women's rights in countries that treat women as second-class citizens or worse; insist on the right of women to education and to birth control; make sure that children are not used as suicide murderers, human shields, or targets for incitement; exclude from the medical community anyone who uses medical facilities for terror purposes; limit the flow of incitement emanating from countries who have no free press and no respectable judicial system; and outlaw racist behavior not only within the free world but also everywhere else.

Yes, it's easy to list these things in one long paragraph. It's far more difficult to apply them worldwide. But every intelligent reader knows that the world is moving toward a day when all of these provisions will become necessary. It's just a matter of time until all free countries unite and recognize that they are facing a life-threatening, global problem—and that the answers outlined here are simply the only possible solutions.

In the course of modern history, the civilized world has normally taken a decade or more to go from initial realization to resolute action. It would be a pity to wait so long in this case, when every day another Islamic act of terror is killing and maiming people—while making the lives of hundreds of millions of Muslims less bearable in the process. As long as you can open your TV, radio, newspaper, or website to the news of another round of Islamic terror somewhere in the world, you will know that the free world has not digested the message—and the Muslim world is not yet aware of the destruction it is bringing on itself.

─32─

THE WORLD ACCORDING TO
MY GRANDMOTHER

*I hope that the autobiography of my granddaughter will start
with the words, "My grandfather was an optimist. He was right."*

O ur discussion of the raging storm started with my grandmother
Sarah, herself a third-generation Israeli native. It is time to look
at the future with my other grandmother, Yehudit (the original
Hebrew version of Judith, female form of Judah).

Dr. Chaim Weizmann was the first president of Israel and a successful scientist. Born in a tiny village in Russia, he was sent at the age
of eleven in 1885 to a school in the nearby city of Pinsk. According to
his memoirs, his first impression of the city was a farewell gathering for
the community leader Aharon (same name as the biblical brother of
Moses) Eisenberg. With his pregnant wife and baby daughter in tow,
Eisenberg had decided to immigrate to the land of Israel. The result of
this pregnancy was my grandmother Yehudit, who was born during the
trip to the Promised Land.

In 1890, a few years later, Aharon led a group of Jewish farmers
who purchased a large plot of barren land from its Arab owners, estab-
lishing the community of Rehovot, named after an ancient biblical

town. It is to this same Rehovot that Dr. Weizmann arrived years later and established in 1934 the great research institute carrying his name, building his house on land bought from my grandmother Yehudit. Many years later, I became a scientist at the Weizmann Institute, and later its president.

Yehudit became a teacher. In 1903 she was one of the founders of the teachers' union, the first labor union in Israel. She then married Haim Blumberg, a young, penniless man who had immigrated by himself as a teenager, escaping the Russian custom of drafting thirteen-year-old Jewish boys into the army. Because Eisenberg was a well-known name in the local Jewish community and Blumberg was not, the feminist Yehudit refused to accept her husband's family name. The compromise was to translate the ending "berg" (German for mountain), which appears in both Blumberg and Eisenberg, into Harari, which is Hebrew for "someone from the mountain."

Yehudit lived to the age of ninety-three. She lived to address the seventy-fifth anniversary ceremony of the union she helped establish, and she was a teacher, writer, and a school principal for fifty years. She was born in transit from Tsarist Russia to the Ottoman Empire; grew up in a Jewish village in Israel in the nineteenth century; became a teacher, together with her husband, in the first Hebrew high school in the world; was among the sixty founding families of the city of Tel-Aviv (along with my other grandparents); lost a brother in the Turkish army in World War I, a brother-in-law in the second Palestinian wave of terror in 1929, and a nephew in the 1948 war of independence; was bombed by the Italians in World War II and by the Egyptians in 1948; saw her only son elected to the first Israeli Parliament and serve there for twenty-five years; survived all the wars and terror until after the 1973 Yom Kippur War; and lived to see peace between Israel and Egypt.

I share these bits and pieces of my grandmother's life story in order to generate hope and optimism. At any point in her long life, there was less reason for hope than there is now. There was more trouble, more pressure, more danger, and more pessimism. Israel was less stable, less affluent, and less safe. The Jews were more embattled and hated just as thoroughly. The world was just as full of war and conflict as it is today. There were always one or more madmen who wanted to destroy the civilized world. Nevertheless, we are still here.

At times throughout her life, it must have been difficult to understand how shortsighted the world could be. There was the senseless carnage of World War I; the blindness of the world toward the Nazis in the 1930s; the Holocaust that followed and the silence of the world; the 1948 attack of five countries against the embryonic Israel and the immediate arms embargo imposed on the Jewish state by the entire Western world; the 1967 Egyptian blockade and siege around Israel and the immediate treacherous embargo by the French, the only supplier of Israeli weapons at that time; the traumatic surprise attack by Egypt and Syria in the 1973 war and the resulting advance of the Israeli army, reaching the gates of Damascus and stopping a one-hour drive from Cairo; and, after her death, more waves of Palestinian terror, the descent of Saddam's Scud missiles into Tel Aviv, and a revival of anti-Semitism in Europe.

Yet, during this same period, Israel grew into a modern country. Science, art, literature, and music flourish within its borders. Millions of Jewish refugees have been absorbed with open arms. The country is protected by a strong defense force. Its per capita income is on a par with that of the European countries. Its leaders have signed peace agreements with two of Israel's neighbors. Even the Palestinians themselves now dare to say the name Israel and talk with Israeli leaders. All these wars were won because the first loss would have meant the end of the Jewish state. For Israel, it's clear that the full half of the glass is much more impressive than the empty half. More important, the trend is positive: The glass is growing fuller, not emptier.

And that's not even to mention Israel's first Olympic gold medal ever in the 2004 games at Athens. The Jews, who were rarely involved in manual labor, but excelled in commerce, medicine, music, law, science, and the like, have long been alleged to deal in *Luft Geschaeft*, literally meaning "airy business" in both German and Yiddish. How fitting that the first Israeli Olympic champion earned his gold medal in windsurfing—just as it's the air force that's keeping Israel alive today.

Even the current wave of suicide murders, which appeared to be unstoppable, has subsided when confronted with the triple punch of the defensive barrier, the offensive attacks on the ringleaders, and the excellent intelligence penetration of the murderers' ranks. The world should take note.

Some might suggest, cynically, that the only insurmountable problem in Israel is the Jews themselves. They enjoy quarreling with each other; they nurture chaos, which is part of long Jewish tradition; and they practice nonstop the art of "beating the system." When there are fifteen parties in the parliament, the next order of business is splitting them further, not merging two parties into one. When union leaders are unhappy, whether the reasons are right or wrong, the first thing they do is strike, crippling the harbors and the only airport in this surrounded and embattled country.

On the other hand, the first two leaders of the country, Prime Minister David Ben-Gurion and President Chaim Weizmann—who could not stand each other—agreed that Israel would have no chance unless it gave first priority to science. The result is that the country has become a center for groundbreaking scientific research, impressive high-tech industry, satellite technology, sophisticated agriculture, and a military might that discourages any sensible attacker. Another result is the Weizmann Institute of Science and Ben-Gurion University, named after those two heroes who never got along.

And the global storm? My grandmother was also a citizen of Globania. Optimism is a state of mind, not a profession, and certainly not a national attribute or a mathematical theorem. She watched as the great murderous leaders of her time overextended their ambitions and ended up in defeat, bringing terrible devastation on their own people. The civilized world is often late to react to madness, but even after long periods of denial it always wakes up in time to save itself. Money and greed are important motivating forces, but ultimately danger to life always surpasses them on the priority list. That is why France and the United States have more in common than they themselves believe, and why the Islamic terrorists have no chance to win against the free world. They may score points by murdering, beheading, hijacking, and kidnapping, but in the end they will be defeated. International law will have to be rewritten to prevent future terror and allow the destruction of the networks that support it—until someone finds another method of endangering humanity and exploiting its weaknesses.

The biblical Moses lived to the age of one hundred and twenty. The Jewish tradition is, on every birthday, to wish: "Until one hundred and twenty." Had she lived, my grandmother Yehudit would have turned one hundred and twenty in the year 2005. If she had lived to witness the present raging storm, she would have weathered it. So will we.

ACKNOWLEDGMENTS

My first thanks are to my ancestors who, during the nineteenth century, each in his or her own crazy way, came to a barren and dangerous land, "the eye of the storm," in order to find a place where Jews could take care of themselves. They are responsible for the one line in my CV to which I have contributed nothing: my being fifth-generation Israeli-born.

I am indebted to Victor Halberstadt and Martin Gerstel, who probably do not know each other, but who became the father and the mother of this book. As always, the father was the source at the conception, and the mother gave birth. The fetus was the article, preceding this book. However, in this case, neither of them knew about the existence of the baby book until it was in puberty. Neither Victor nor Martin has seen the book before publication, and it is extremely likely that they do not agree with much of it. These good people should not be blamed for anything.

I thank my agent, Marvin Josephson, who was always correct, especially when he told me, at the beginning, that he is a stubborn man. Without his stubbornness, this book would not have happened, and the baby would not have reached school age. Calvert Morgan, my editor, in an extraordinary display of ability, speed, and patience, added more than just cosmetics and good English to the growing child. Both of them have been invaluable.

Many dear friends, especially Bob Asher, Lester Crown, Bill Davidson, Maurice Dwek, and Mandy Moross, were instrumental in encouraging me to write the book and in helping to spread the word. I appreciate your trust and value your friendship.

I also thank the many hundreds of strangers who wrote to me about the precursor article, praised it, encouraged me, and almost demanded a book version. They—as well as the Pakistani journalist who quoted most of the article in his magazine, the Korean newspaper which glorified me as "a strategist," the American military attaché to an Arab country who wrote to me, and the Brazilian gentleman who translated it to Portuguese—all served as proof that when you tell it like it is, people listen.

Finally, nothing would have happened or could have happened, without my wife Elfi, the European ambassador to my life, who has become an ambassador from the eye of the storm to the world.

INDEX

A

Abdullah bin Al-Hussein, King of
  Jordan, 65
Afghanistan, 15, 69
  financing terrorists, 196
  as terrorist supporter, 202
  treatment of women, 196
Air France, hijacked flight, 177
Al Aksa, 188
Al Jazeera, 116, 119
al Qaida, 12, 17, 18, 68, 76
Al-Manar, 116, 204
al-Sahaf, Mohammed Saeed, 114
al-Salahiat, Abu Muhammad, 133
Algeria
  as a neighbor to Israel, 62
  murders in, 12
American Civil Liberties Union, 32
American experience with war,
  72–74
Amnesty International, 32
anti-European sentiment, 72
anti-Semitism, 76, 81, 99, 117, 179
  and Israel, 175, 178
  and the United Nations, 93,
    176–177
apartheid, 117

apathy to terrorism, 101
appeasement, price of, 100
Arab lands:
  compared with Israel, 152
  size and population of, 11, 13
Arab population, age of, 119
Arab solidarity, 62
Arab world:
  birth rates in, 13
  Gross Domestic Product of, 53–54
  publications in, 13
Arafat, Yasir, 60–61, 115, 117, 141,
    144, 155, 188–189, 201–203
  family of, 188
  and Syria, 60
  unable to stop terrorism, 202
Assad, Hafez, 164

B

Bangladesh, a Muslim nation, 66
BBC, 119
Begin, Menachem, 59
Ben-Gurion, David, 210
bin Laden, Osama, 115, 186

biological weapons, 196
birth rates in Arab world, 13
Blumberg, Haim, 207–208
Bremer, Paul, 26
Buchanan, Pat, 88, 95
Bush, George W., 72, 88

C

Carter, Jimmy, 59
chemical warfare, 196
China:
    economy of, 82–83
    views on Jews, 80
Chinese, overseas, 79, 85
Chirac, Jacques, 72
civilians, killing, 34–37
Clinton, Bill, 187
CNN, 26, 110, 119, 125

D

de Villepin, Dominique, 72, 76
democracy, opposition to, 17–21
Diaspora, use of term, 79

E

East Asian Muslim countries, 84
education, role of, 51–52
Egypt, demographics of, 59

Eisenberg, Aharon, 207–208
Eisenberg, Yehudit, 207–208
Electronic Revolution, 48
environmental organizations,
    92
Erakat, Saeb , 202
Europe, Muslim immigrants in,
    75–76
European:
    apathy to terrorism, 101
    attitude toward war,
        74–75
    Left, 91, 95, 115
extremism, 87

F

Fatah movement, 202
Foul, Khalil Abu, 133
freedom:
    academic, 93
    of press, 105
    of religion, 105, 106, 155
    of speech, 106

G

Garibaldi, Giuseppe, 143
Gaza Strip, Egyptian control
    of, 153
genetic revolution, 54
Geneva Convention, 35

Genome Project, 54
global terrorism, 33
global village, 49
globalization:
    evidence of, 49
    used by terrorists, 21
Globania:
    contrasted with Israel, 181
    deal with Israel, 156
    defining, 39–40
    economics of, 47–48
Goebbels, Joseph, 114
Golan Heights, 172
Green Line, 157, 160–161, 172,
    192–193
Gross Domestic Product (GDP), 13,
    48–50, 53–54, 59, 81, 82, 181,
    182

massacre, 152
hijacked planes, 99, 177
Hitler, Adolf, 37, 88, 100, 105, 152,
    163, 164, 170
Hizbullah, 17, 18, 21, 60, 68, 76,
    116, 170
    control of Iran, 203
    as drug producer, 203
    in Lebanon, 203
    supplied by Syria, 203
Holocaust, 81, 89, 95, 115, 118,
    138, 143, 144, 164, 170, 175,
    209
human rights issues, 13
Hussein, Saddam, 4, 12, 26, 48, 61,
    72, 89, 114, 185, 209
Hussein bin Talal, King of Jordan,
    59, 186, 188

H

I

Ha'aretz, 41
Haider, Jeorg, 62, 89, 95
Hamas, 71, 60, 68, 76–77, 110, 138,
    163, 170, 201
    in Syria, 60
Harari, Dina, 4
Harari, Haim, 34
    biographical details, 3–5
Harari, Izhar, 34
Harari, Moshe, 152
Harari, Sarah, 3
Harari, Yehudit, 207–208, 211
Harari, Yocheved, 3
Hebron, 90

immigrants, Muslim, 67, 75–76
immigration:
    Jewish, 117, 146, 147, 181, 182
    laws, 19, 51
Indonesia, a Muslim nation, 66
Information Age, 48, 54–55
Intellectual Property Revolution,
    53–54
International Court of Justice, 38,
    42–43
International Herald Tribune, 123
international law:
    rewriting, 33–38
    and terrorists, 195, 204, 211

International Red Cross, 38, 125,
126
symbol of, 42
Internet:
effects of, 8–10
and false reporting, 107
terrorist use of, 21, 194
intifada, 4, 125, 187
Iran:
demographics of, 66–67
nuclear program, 197
and support of terrorism, 68–69,
197, 202
terrorism, 196
as terrorist state, 186
Iran-Iraq war, 12, 37
Iraq war:
Europe's role in, 72
opposition of, 115
Iraq, 63, 65
under Saddam Hussein, 185
as terrorist supporter, 202
U.S. attack on, 69
Islam, 66
Islamic fanaticism, in Turkey, 67
Islamic Jihad, 17, 68, 170
Islamic terror, 67, 77, 89, 97, 101,
106, 197, 205
war against, 195
Islamophobia, 14, 75, 76, 89
Israel:
annihilation of, 170
Arab terror waves, 152
borders of, 154
demographics of, 182, 184
demonizing, 76
experience with war, 73

far Left, 88
far Right, 90
genocide accusation, 163–164
neighbors of, 59–63
nuclear capability, 198
Palestinian border disputes, 157
the people of, 183
politics, 183
as a racist state, 117
response to Palestinian terror, 94,
123
right wing, 89
Sinai War, 156
size and population of, 11
as underdog, 163
unrecognized war with Arabs,
153
wall with Palestine, 117, 125, 160
West Bank settlement, 89
Israeli:
army, 122
ambulance searches, 125, 126
border checkpoints, 132
citizens murdered, 201
Israeli-Palestinian conflict, 169, 172,
195
conclusion of, 192–191

J

Jaffa murders, 152
Japan:
economy of, 81
views on Jews, 80
Jenin refugee camp, 138–139

history of, 160
Israeli attack on, 161
as terror center, 161
Jerusalem:
    as Jewish capital, 191
    old city of, 194
    as Palestinian capital, 155
Jews, as targets, 88
Jews in Israel, origins of, 6–7
Jordan:
    allied with Egypt, 186
    annexation of the West Bank,
        153
    demographics of, 61
    host of Arafat, 186
    supporter of Saddam Hussein,
        186

K

Kerry, John, 88
Khodary, El, 134
Khomeini revolution, 68
Kurds, 70, 94, 196
Kuwait, invasion of, 12

L

Le Monde, 41
Lebanon, demographics of, 60
    Hizbullah in, 60–61
    Muslim-Christian war in, 12

Libya, 13, 40
    as terrorist supporter, 202
    bombing of Pan Am, 12, 103

M

Meir, Golda, 8
Middle East, background, 58–59
Moussa, Amr, 63
Muslim Brothers, 88
Muslim nations, 66
Muslim-Christian war, 12
Myre, Greg, 133

N

Nasser, Gamal Abdel, 186
NATO, 66
New York Times, 11, 41,
    132–136
    fallacies in report, 134
Nobel Peace Prize, 62
Nongovernmental organizations
    (NGOs), 94
Nuclear weapons, 197

O

Oil for Food Program, 48
Oslo agreements, 187, 188
Ottoman Empire, 6

P

Pakistan, as a Muslim nation, 66
Palestine:
  authority of, 157, 188
  British offer of partition, 186
  European support of, 188
  fictitious history, 145
  Green Line creating ghetto, 160
  harming itself, 188
  historic population density,
    146–148
  history of, 144–145
  Israeli border disputes, 157
  Jewish settlements in, 147–148,
    157
  and Jordan and Lebanon, 61–62
  lies of, 159
  origins of, 7
  post-Arafat leadership, 189
  rewriting history, 155
  right of return as bargaining chip,
    172
  support of Hitler, 152
  terror campaigns of the 1950s,
    154
  terrorism in, 201
  as underdog, 95, 152
Palestine Liberation Organization,
  156, 186
Pan Am 103, bombing of, 12, 103
paradoxes, 31–32, 48–49, 50
peace in the Middle East, 191
press:
  Arab television, 108, 116, 124,
    203
  checks and balances, 107–108
  coverage of Jenin refugee camp,
    160
  distortion of Israeli-Palestinian
    situation, 131
  distortion of truth, 107, 109,
    118–119
  intimidation of, 109–110
  misleading pictures, 121–127
  Palestinian cameramen, 122
  response to intimidation, 110
  as terrorist weapon, 113
  Western dependence on locals,
    108
profiling, 98
Protocols of the Elders of Zion, The,
  81
proverbial taxi driver:
  definition of, xii
  misinformed, 131
publications in Arab world, 13

Q

Qaddafi, Muammar, 62, 89
Qatar, as broadcaster of Arab
  television, 203

R

Rabin, Yitzhak, 59, 90
racism, United Nations resolution
  against, 176

radioactive bombs, 197
Rashomon, 4
Red Crescent, 42, 125–126, 133
Red Lion, 42
refugee camps, 140
refugees, 137
    Jenin Palestinian camp, 138–139
    Jewish, 138
    Palestinian, 137–138
    resettlement of, 192
religious fanaticism, 56
Reuters, 110
Russia, 70

S

Sadat, Anwar, 59
Salah-ad-Din, 143
Salim, Ahmed, 130
Saudi Arabia:
    financing terrorists, 196
    as Islamic organization financier,
        203
    support of terrorism, 186
    and terrorism, 63
    treatment of women, 196
    victim of terrorism, 186
Saudis, killed by al Qaida, 12
science, as an asset, 55
security measures:
    at airports, 97
    at Israeli public places, 98
September 11, 24, 27, 68, 76, 77, 99,
    100, 114, 115, 131, 134, 136,
    144, 185

Sharon, Ariel, 88, 134, 141, 147
Shiite Muslims, 155
Shiite terrorists, 60–61, 68
South Korea, economy of, 81
Star of David, 42
Sudan:
    demographics of, 62–63
    genocide in, 63, 94
    mass murder in, 12
suicide murders, 5, 23, 118, 202,
    205, 210
    barrier to, 42–43
    children as, 26, 37, 44, 115,
        205
    Europe and, 27, 76
    factors behind, 25
    factors creating, 14
    financing of, 48, 116, 188
    in Iraq, 24, 111
    as Islamic terror, 185
    in Israel, 99, 123, 161
    Israeli wall and, 42–43, 117, 125,
        160
    in Madrid, 76
    and no defense, 25, 43
    Palestinian, 24, 30–31, 48, 177,
        197, 202
    punishment for, 6, 33, 35, 40,
        195, 198
    refugee camps and, 140
    religious leaders and, 20, 105
    the United Nations and, 40, 43,
        163
Sunni Hamas, 68
Syria:
    host to terrorists, 60
    supplier of Hizbullah, 203

T

Taliban, 12
Technology Revolution, 54–55, 82
terrorism:
    diagnosing, 204
    planning, 20–21
    solution to, 205
    specific acts of, 23–24, 26–27
    supporting, 48
terrorists:
    as criminals, 204
    hosts of, 60
    tactics of, 122–125
    weapons of, 113, 196
Turkey:
    demographics of, 66–67, 69, 70
    EU issues, 76, 91

U

United Nations:
    Israel and, 40
    member of, 40
United Nations Durban Conference
    (2001), 93, 95, 177
United Nations General Assembly,
    40, 63, 176
United Nations High Commissioner
    on Refugees (UNHCR), 138

United Nations Human Rights
    Commission, 13, 20, 39, 40
United Nations Relief and Work
    Agency (UNRWA), 138
United Nations Security Council,
    20, 40, 61, 164
United States:
    attack on Iraq, 69
    as superpower, 77
    (See specific topics.)

W

Weizmann, Chaim, 207–208, 210
West Bank, 192
    Jewish settlement of, 89
    and Jordan, 61
women:
    Muslim treatment of, 92
    organizations of, 91, 92
    social status of, 13
words:
    as propaganda, 114
    as weapons, 113

Y

Yeman, murders in, 12
Yom Kippur War, 208